D1261023

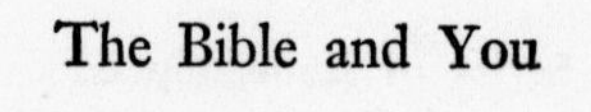
The Bible and You

THE COOPERATIVE SERIES

LEADERSHIP TRAINING TEXTS

Many thousands of lay workers in Protestant Churches attend interdenominational leadership education schools each year. It is essential that the courses offered and the text materials used be acceptable to the many varieties of Protestant groups found in our American communities.

The Cooperative Series of leadership education textbooks are produced to meet that need. They are planned by the Division of Christian Education of the National Council of the Churches of Christ in the U.S.A., representing thirty-nine Protestant denominations. The Cooperative Publication Association, an interdenominational group of denominational editors and publishers, selects the writers and provides editorial supervision to insure sound educational values, practical usefulness and interdenominational approval and acceptance.

EDWARD P. BLAIR

The BIBLE and YOU

A Guide for Reading the Bible in the Revised Standard Version

PUBLISHED FOR

The Cooperative Publication Association

BY

ABINGDON PRESS

New York *Nashville*

THE BIBLE AND YOU

Library of Congress Catalog Card Number: 53-6348

F

SET UP, PRINTED, AND BOUND BY THE PARTHENON PRESS, AT NASHVILLE, TENNESSEE, UNITED STATES OF AMERICA

In gratitude
for
the friendship and distinguished service of four Garrett colleagues

Horace Greeley Smith	Harris Franklin Rall
Edmund D. Soper	Arthur W. Nagler

Preface

TODAY, AS NEVER BEFORE, THE BIBLE AND YOU STAND FACE TO FACE. IT CONFRONTS YOU EVERYWHERE YOU LOOK. You see it in your hotel room, in window displays, in the public library, on the mantel in the home of a friend. Passages from it appear on billboards and car cards. A portion of it may be thrust into your hands as you are walking down the street. You hear it read over the radio and see it fingered lovingly by television preachers. When you go to a political rally, you find candidates alluding to its precepts. In church you hear it extolled by preachers and Sunday-school teachers. Across the table in a restaurant you observe a bulging G.I. pocket from which protrudes a copy of the New Testament.

When you travel abroad, you do not escape the ever-present Bible. It is estimated that more than twenty million copies and portions, printed in eleven hundred languages and dialects, are distributed each year throughout the world. Distribution is continuing in Communist countries. In free lands Bible societies are handing out copies by the millions.

You can read the Bible in many English translations. The King James Version of 1611 is still used by multitudes of Americans and Britons, in spite of its archaic expressions. Others prefer the English Revised Version or its American counterpart, the American Standard Version, of 1881 and 1901 respectively. Modern versions by individual translators, like Moffatt, Goodspeed, and Weymouth, have their devotees. And now a new revision, the Revised Standard Version, offers you a remarkable combination of the stately language of the King James Version and the simple, direct, and up-to-date vocabulary of the one-man renditions, with more scholarly accuracy than in any previous version. It is certainly destined to win its way into ever larger acceptance by individuals and the churches, until it becomes the standard American version.

There are Bibles available today in practically every kind of print, format, and binding. If you are conservative in your tastes, you may have the Bible in conventional black covers with red- or gilt-edged pages. If you prefer the modern look, you can have it in colored binding with plain pages. If your eyesight is going or gone, you can secure the Bible in Braille. It can be purchased in expensive or cheap editions, and millions of copies are given away. The Bible is the most available book in the world today.

The significance of this world-wide circulation of the Bible can hardly be grasped. In the race for control of the future the free men will outdistance the enslaved largely, perhaps, because of the impetus afforded by this book. The news commentator Lowell Thomas once remarked, "The Bible is of vital importance in teaching freedom. . . . Dictators fear the Bible—and for good reason. It inspired the Magna Charta and the Declaration of Independence."

Though the Bible is not the easiest book in the world to read and understand, multitudes in all walks of life are finding in it guidance and strength "for the living of these days." Our servicemen discovered during the last great war that many natives of the South Sea Islands loved this book more than life itself; and the noted professor of English literature, William Lyon Phelps, found its study so rewarding that he claimed that "a knowledge of the Bible without a college course is more valuable than a college course without a knowledge of the Bible." Experience has shown that the Bible and most of the classics of world literature are not beyond the comprehension of the ordinary reader. A scholar who has long promoted study of the classics among average adult Americans has said, "It is my honest belief that *almost all of the great books in every field are within the grasp of all normally intelligent men*, on the condition, of course, that they acquire the skill necessary for reading them and make the effort." [1]

It is the purpose of this book to help you—the "normally intelligent" person—acquire greater skill in reading and understanding the Bible. *You* will have to supply the effort. The book makes no attempt to tell you all you ought to know about the Bible: about its origin, contents, transmission, translation, and influence. It does not contain a description of the Revised Standard Version.[2] It assumes that you will read the preface to this version and perhaps parts of the detailed introductions prepared by the Revision Committee.[3] It is rather a laboratory manual—literally a *guide*—to help you in firsthand experimentation in the Bible. My point of view has been well put by Walter Russell Bowie, who has said that the best guide in Bible reading is the person who "does not try to say too much. He tells the inquirer what lies ahead of him if he wants to look, and

[1] Mortimer J. Adler, *How to Read a Book* (New York: Simon and Schuster, Inc., 1940), p. 30. Italics Adler's.

[2] Hereafter referred to as the R.S.V.

[3] Luther A. Weigle (Chairman) and Members of the Revision Committee, *An Introduction to the Revised Standard Version of the New Testament* and *An Introduction to the Revised Standard Version of the Old Testament* (New York: Thomas Nelson and Sons, 1946 and 1952).

how he can get to the vantage point at which the wonders of the Bible will most fully make him open his own eyes." [4]

The heart of this book (Chapters III-VII) consists of a description and application of fundamental procedures in reading the Bible. It is hardly to be hoped that all of you will carry out every direction there given. But you will know the path, and you can follow as far as your time, strength, and interest will allow. At the beginning of the book there are two important chapters on the basic nature of the Bible and generally accepted principles of interpretation. The final chapter contains information concerning some of the best contemporary books about the Bible.

While the procedures set forth in this book are meant primarily for use by individual readers of the Bible, it may be pointed out that study groups can use them with equal success. If all members will follow the directions on the same biblical book and share and compare their insights at group meetings, a rich experience will result for all.

Frequent reference will be found to A.B.C., *The Abingdon Bible Commentary*.[5] This one-volume commentary on the whole Bible is so helpful that you can hardly afford to be without it. Members of study groups may wish to gather together a small library for use by the participants. Several copies of A.B.C. should be included.

It will be obvious to some that at many places in this book I am indebted to professors under whom I have studied at The Biblical Seminary in New York and at Yale University Divinity School. I wish to take this opportunity to express to them my deep appreciation for their brilliant

[4] In Walter D. Ferguson, *Journey Through the Bible* (New York: Harper and Bros., 1947), p. ix.

[5] See p. 147.

instruction and abiding inspiration. Especial thanks are due Dr. Harris Franklin Rall, Dr. Otto J. Baab, and Dr. Vartan D. Melconian for reading the manuscript and offering valuable suggestions. The latter, a friend of many years and companion on a journey to the lands of the Bible, encouraged me in undertaking this project. Gratitude should be expressed also to Dean Emeritus Luther A. Weigle for his kindness in allowing me to consult the page proofs of the R.S.V. of the Old Testament ahead of its publication date.

EDWARD P. BLAIR

Contents

I. [illegible]

II. [illegible]

III. [illegible] 42

IV. [illegible] 74

V. [illegible] 104

VI. [illegible] 147

VII. [illegible]

VIII. [illegible]

Contents

I. The Basic Nature of the Bible 15

II. How to Understand the Bible 31

III. Reading a Book as a Whole 52

IV. Examining the Parts and Re-viewing the Whole 71

V. Reading the Nonunified Books 94

VI. Applying the Methods of Reading 117

VII. Programs of Reading 140

VIII. Resources for Reading 146

Reading Suggestions and Questions for Discussion 151

CHAPTER ONE

The Basic Nature of the Bible

MOST OF YOU HAVE STRUGGLED THROUGH THE AXIOMS OF GEOMETRY. YOU WILL REMEMBER THAT AXIOMS ARE SELF-evident truths, principles that are universally accepted. If one builds a bridge or erects a building in defiance of them, the structure will surely fall.

Axioms are to be found not only in mathematics but in every other field of knowledge. There are even biblical axioms, from which you must start in reading and interpreting the Bible. Ignoring or disdaining them can lead only to confusion compounded.

AXIOM I: *The Bible is a library of books.*

Today the Bible is published between the lids of one covering, so that it looks like a single book. In reality it consists of a great collection of books—sixty-six in number, as they now lie in our Protestant versions—written by many men in many periods of history. Some of the writers were separated from one another by as much as a thousand years. The message of the various books is carried in a variety of literary forms. These forms (songs and other poetic material, historical narrative, laws, prophetic oracles, wise sayings, short stories, letters, apocalypses, etc.) were commonly used in the periods during which the authors wrote.

Furthermore, some books of the Bible are themselves little libraries. The book of Psalms consists of a great collection of smaller collections of psalms. Certain psalms were probably composed almost a thousand years apart.[1] The book of Proverbs, as is evident from the headings to chapters 30 and 31, is likewise made up of collections of varying dates. The books of the great prophets, like Isaiah and Jeremiah, contain sermons preached by them, autobiographical and biographical materials (the latter penned by their followers), and prophecies composed by other men who lived long after their time.[2] It might be said that the books of the Pentateuch are individually little libraries, for it is now known that their authors joined together written sources to form our present connected narratives.[3]

The Bible is a massive collection of collections, a book of amazing scope and variety. This is one of the secrets of its universal appeal. In reading and interpreting it, it is very important that you remember that it is a highly complex library rather than a single unified work. Exactly why this is of consequence will appear later.

AXIOM II: *The Bible is a library of related books.*

Though the books of the Bible were written by many men in varying periods of history and thus, for the most part, originally existed independently of one another, they

[1] See A.B.C., pp. 510, 513.

[2] *Ibid.*, pp. 679-80.

[3] *Ibid.*, pp. 134-44.

have many things in common. Their authors were almost without exception Hebrews, or Jews, who left upon their creations clear marks of a common culture. One of the major features of this culture was a concern with God's redemptive activity in behalf of men.

Hebrew religion passed through many stages in its long history, but certain dominant emphases continued through virtually all its changes. The belief that God had chosen the Hebrews for his own possession and that he had entered into a covenant with them involving obligations on their part and on his, lay at the heart of the religious faith of early biblical writers. At length it was believed that God was active in Israel's experience to bring not only his chosen people but other nations as well into holy fellowship with him. The writers of the New Testament see Jesus of Nazareth as God's unique instrument in effecting the long-awaited redemption of men. They regard all that led up to him as a preparation by God for the coming of his Son.

It is fair to say that the Bible contains one long story, a story that embraces the whole universe and all time. It deals with God's attempt to bring into being a people with whom he might enter into intimate, holy fellowship and the realization of this purpose at last through Jesus Christ. The Bible clearly contains no haphazard collection of miscellaneous books but rather books that are related in some way to a single theme—the saving work of God.

Axiom III: *The Bible is a library of ancient books.*

At times passages of the Bible speak so directly to our hearts that it seems as if the authors were writing just for us. It is easy to forget that the Bible has a long history behind it, and that many people in many periods of time have found this wonderful book ministering to their needs. Chief among these, of course, were the first readers.

An observant person soon discovers that many of the books indicate for whom they were originally written. The letters of Paul open with a salutation in which the identity of the first readers is given: "Paul, . . . to all God's beloved in Rome"; "Paul, . . . to the church of God which is at Corinth."

When the contents of the letters are examined, it is soon apparent that Paul was dealing with practical problems which these churches were facing; he was not addressing himself to our problems today. Morton Scott Enslin underscores the point when he says that if Paul had possessed a magic carpet, he would not have written his letters at all.[4] Harris Franklin Rall characterizes Paul's objective in writing in words which would apply to all the biblical writers: "He is not writing with the thought that posterity is looking over his shoulder."[5]

It often takes considerable searching to discover the original readers and the purpose for which many of the biblical books were written, for these facts are not always stated. Many today regard the book of Daniel, for example, as a prophecy of events of our times, written in order that we may know when to expect the end of the world. Modern scholarship has shown that the book was really composed for Jews of the second century B.C. who were suffering at the hands of a self-deifying Syrian tyrant, Antiochus Epiphanes, and his confederates. It was meant to encourage them to remain faithful to their God and their religious duties by pointing out that God has a way of unseating

[4] *Christian Beginnings* (New York: Harper & Bros., 1938), p. 213.

[5] *According to Paul* (New York: Charles Scribner's Sons, 1944), p. 9.

impious dictators, and that he will vindicate his worshipers by giving them victory over their persecutors if they but wait patiently for him. This message is, of course, applicable to persecuted, God-fearing people of every age, but it was addressed by the author to people of his own time.

Even First and Second Chronicles, so-called historical books, have discoverable first readers and original purposes. From a comparison with the books of Samuel and Kings, on which the chronicler has based much of his narrative, it is apparent that the latter has rewritten Hebrew history from a priestly point of view. He is interested in showing how the ritual and institutions of the temple of his day came into being, how the authority of Israel's great leaders stands behind these practices, and how God himself ordained them. The vocabulary of the author, his style of writing, the fact that he bases his account on Samuel-Kings, and his glorification of the temple institutions and ritual—all lead scholars to the conclusion that he meant to stimulate loyalty to and pride in the temple on the part of his Jerusalem contemporaries in the third century B.C. That there is material of value in his books for us today is a matter of gratification. But we must not suppose that he had us in mind when he wrote.

We must remember also that we hold in our hands today a Bible which has a hoary textual history. Countless persons of many generations and nationalities perpetuated it as a living book by making copies of it. The original manuscripts soon perished, for they consisted of material of short durability in most climates—animal skins and papyrus. Today we possess some 4,500 Greek manuscripts of the New Testament of various ages and from various countries. About eight hundred manuscripts of the Hebrew Old Testament have been examined by scholars. When manuscripts are compared, one finds that occasionally they present striking textual variations in the same passages. It was inevitable that scribes should copy incorrectly at times. The eye does not always see accurately, and the hand grows numb and inept.

Scholars have been at work for about 250 years comparing all available manuscripts, including the new ones discovered from time to time, in the attempt to recover as far as possible the text of the various books as they left the hands of their authors. Their results are now fully incorporated in the R.S.V. In this version we may rest assured that we have a substantially accurate text. Some passages that appear in the King James Version of 1611 have been left out,[6] and some have been altered,[7] on the basis of convincing manuscript evidence that has come to light since 1611. However, such changes need cause us little concern. On the authority of Frederick C. Grant, who speaks for the New Testament revisers, "no doctrine of the Christian faith has been affected by the revision, for the simple reason that, out of the thousands of variant readings in the manuscripts, none has turned up thus far that requires a revision of Christian doctrine." [8] The result of all this scholarly research has been pure gain. We have a finer and more reliable Bible today than ever before in Christian history.

In view of the fact that the books of the Bible were addressed originally to ancient readers and have behind them a long history of textual transmission, we can hardly

[6] E.g., Mark 16:9-20; Luke 22:19*b*, 20; John 5:4; 7:53–8:11; Acts 8:37. They are printed in the footnotes in small type.

[7] E.g., Mark 1:2; Luke 4:44; John 9:35.

[8] Luther A. Weigle and Members of the Revision Committee, *An Introduction to the Revised Standard Version of the New Testament*, p. 42.

open the Bible at random, especially in one of the older versions, and expect to find a message addressed directly to us. To treat the Bible in this way is to disregard an important axiom. Exactly how the Bible does speak to us will become apparent later.

AXIOM IV: *The Bible is a library of oriental books.*

The literature of a nation inevitably bears the marks of the nation's culture. Culture is the product of many factors, not the least of which are climate, geography, and topography. The little land that gave birth to the Bible was so located and so constituted that it fell within the orbit of that type of culture which we label oriental.

Ancient oriental culture is not easy to characterize in a few words. Some of its features may, however, be distinguished and commented on briefly.

1. Blood relationships were strongly stressed and jealously guarded. The tribe, consisting of a group of closely related families, was the basic social unit. Marriages were to be contracted only within certain prescribed limits, in order that the tribal blood be not polluted. Land belonging to members of the tribe could not be sold to outsiders but was passed down from generation to generation within the tribe. Pride of ancestry and tribal history was pronounced. Genealogies were kept and proudly recited. Bedouins of the Jordan region still sit around campfires and recite genealogies to the delight of all. One does not read far in the Old Testament—or the New, for that matter—until he comes across many evidences of tribal culture.

2. Nomadism, while not the only form of socio-economic organization in the ancient Orient, was widely prevalent. Tribal groups migrated from place to place with their flocks,

from which they derived almost their entire livelihood.

The nomadic way of life has left its imprint almost everywhere in the Bible—in the content of its stories, its language, and its symbolism. God is the psalmist's "shepherd." To Ezekiel, Israel's rulers are evil shepherds who do not feed the sheep and bind up their wounds. God himself will therefore shepherd his sheep. In the Gospel of John, Jesus is "the good shepherd" who "lays down his life for the sheep." According to the book of Revelation "the Lamb in the midst of the throne will be [the] shepherd" of the righteous and "will guide them to springs of living water." The practice of offering animal sacrifices goes back to Israel's nomadic days. The significance of these sacrifices, so obvious to the ancient nomad, is lost on a modern city-bred child or adult who knows nothing about the customs of nomadic peoples. It is understandably difficult for us to comprehend the sacrificial language of both Testaments.

3. The ancient oriental mind was highly reflective. It delighted in creating and reciting pithy, salty utterances (proverbs, riddles, fables, and parables) in which explanations of the curious phenomena of life, observations on the meaning of life, and counsels on conduct in life were offered. Vast amounts of such material were passed down from generation to generation. The largest single body of it in the Bible is now to be found in the book of Proverbs, though the historical books, the prophetic books, the Gospels, and the epistles present sizable amounts of it. These materials comprise one of the most valuable strata of the Bible. In them the centuries seem to speak to the moment with ripe counsels.

4. Ancient oriental language was picturesque, nonscien-

tific language. It abounded in metaphors, hyperboles, symbolism, and the like.

A metaphor may be defined as the "use of a word or phrase literally denoting one kind of object or idea in place of another by way of suggesting a likeness or analogy between them." [9] Our modern advertising makes large use of metaphors. For example, an advertisement of a certain motor oil features a cat crouching expectantly near a mousehole, with the comment: "Stays on the job." Another for the same product portrays a ferocious-looking bulldog and adds: "Just naturally tough."

This carry-over of ideas and language is particularly necessary when one is talking about psychic and religious experiences. "Earth has no net of language in which to snare the skies." When a person habitually makes wise decisions and pronouncements, we call him a *deep* thinker, and if the contrary is true, a *shallow* thinker. We talk about a problem *on* the mind or *under* consideration. Thought, literally, has no dimensions, nor can it be localized. In popular speech we sometimes describe a moment of fear by saying, "My heart sank within me," or "My blood ran cold." John Wesley described his conversion experience by saying that his heart was "strangely warmed." The Bible's physical psychology is similar to these modern nonscientific conceptions. The heart is regarded as the seat of intelligence, the bowels of pity, the nostrils of anger, the eye of greed or generosity. It is hardly to be expected that the Bible should furnish us with scientifically defensible concepts and terminology.

The extent to which biblical language is saturated with

[9] *Webster's New International Dictionary of the English Language* (Springfield, Mass.: G. & C. Merriam Co., 1950).

metaphors is not commonly realized. When we call God "Father" or "King," we are carrying over experience from one realm to another. The Psalms abound in metaphorical expressions, such as "The Lord is my rock, and my fortress." What we really mean is that God does for us in the spiritual realm what a rock and a fortress do in the physical. Jeremiah is using a metaphor when he represents God as saying, "I will put my law within them, and I will write it upon their hearts." When Jesus is said to be "the Son of God," "the Lamb of God," "the last Adam," "the pioneer of their salvation," "a great priest over the house of God"; when Christians are called "children of light," "a holy temple in the Lord," "a royal priesthood," Christ's "body"; when truth, righteousness, and faith are represented as a girdle, a breastplate, and a shield, and the complete spiritual endowment "the whole armor of God"; when the final dwelling place of the righteous is called "Mount Zion . . . the city of the living God, the heavenly Jerusalem," "the city which has foundations, whose builder and maker is God"—we are in the realm of metaphorical language. There is no other way in which man can describe the indescribable. A recognition of the deeply metaphorical nature of all language will keep us alert to biblical metaphors and save us from narrow literalism in many of our interpretations.

Hyperboles are overstatements made for the sake of striking effect. Illustrative are some of the sayings of Jesus: "It is easier for a camel to go through the eye of a needle than for a rich man to enter the kingdom of God"; and "Whoever says to this mountain, 'Be taken up and cast into the sea,' and does not doubt in his heart, but believes that what he says will come to pass, it will be done for him." Let us look at the former for a moment. That it was not absolutely impossible for a rich person to get into the kingdom of God seems to be evident from the fact that "Joanna, the wife of Chuza, Herod's steward," who helped to support Jesus and his disciples and who obviously was a woman of wealth, was accepted as a regular member of Jesus' company of followers (Luke 8:1-3). Zacchaeus' wealth did not unconditionally bar him from the kingdom of God, though he did presumably give much of it up (Luke 19:1-10). The saying exaggerates in a striking way to make the perils of wealth unmistakably evident. Here again literalism is unjustified.

Symbolic language is strikingly used in the two apocalypses of the Bible, Daniel and Revelation. These were underground writings, circulated in times of persecution. By the use of symbolic language (beasts, number symbols like 666, a drunken harlot, a dragon, etc.) the oppressors and their demonic confederates could be alluded to and their downfall predicted without danger to writer and readers.

A full-scale treatment of the orientalisms of the Bible would require an entire book. Perhaps enough has been said here to make you aware of the importance of understanding the culture out of which the Bible came in interpreting it.

AXIOM V: *The Bible is a library of selected books.*

When Roman Catholic and Protestant Bibles are compared, one discovers in the former many books not contained in the latter. These books are known as apocryphal books. They were present in the Greek version of the Old Testament used in Alexandria and other cities of the Greco-Roman world at the time of the rise of Christianity, but not in the Hebrew Old Testament. When the Latin translation of the Bible, known as the Vulgate, was made by Jerome about A.D. 400, the apocryphal books were included. They have remained in the Catholic Bible to this day. Martin Luther, a careful student of Hebrew, knew that they were not in the Hebrew Bible. Critical of their contents, as well as aware of their absence from the canon as officially determined by orthodox Judaism, he gathered them together from their respective positions among the officially recognized books and placed them in a sort of appendix to the Old Testament. The apocryphal books were at first included in the King James Bible, but the Puritans objected so strongly to the morals of some of these books that they were soon left out. Most Protestants know little about them.

In addition to the books of the Apocrypha many other books circulated among the Jews of the intertestamental period. These books, known today as the Pseudepigrapha ("false writings," so called because they falsely claim to have been written by famous men of the past), were probably avidly read in some circles. However, they were accepted in neither the Greek nor the Hebrew canons. The discovery in 1947 of a cave near the Dead Sea, in which many ancient manuscripts were cached, has added several books to our library of noncanonical works.[10]

There are apocrypha of the New Testament as well as of the Old. These Christian writings circulated more or less widely from the second to the fourth centuries A.D. Some of them were considered so valuable that they were

[10] See *The Biblical Archaeologist* (New Haven: American Schools of Oriental Research), vol. XI, no. 3 (Sept., 1948), and vol. XII, nos. 2, 3 (May and Sept., 1949) and Madeleine S. and J. Lane Miller, *Harper's Bible Dictionary* (New York: Harper & Bros., 1952), pp. 653-55.

accepted as canonical by prominent churches. Others were obviously of inferior quality and were never regarded very seriously. It was not until the fourth century that it was finally decided exactly which Christian books should be accepted as authoritative, though most of them had made their way to the fore long before this. Most of those now present in our New Testament commended themselves to the Christian consciousness over a long period of time. With one or two exceptions their superiority is obvious when one compares them with their rivals. Christians have long believed that the Spirit of God guided the church in its selection, and modern scholarship attests the wisdom of its choice.

These dozens of noncanonical books are of great value to students of the Bible. They help us understand the times out of which the biblical books came: the ideas and language of the various periods, the literary forms popular in these periods, the course of events, and so on. Countless verses of the Bible are illuminated by passages in these outside books. But, for all their value, the light of God's revelation shines but dimly through most of them, and they rightly take second or third place in the great redemptive literature of the Judaeo-Christian tradition.

AXIOM VI: *The Bible is a library of redemptive books.*

Our discussion of the basic nature of the Bible would fall far short of the church's traditional view of it if we were to conclude with Axiom V. Up to this point we have looked at the Bible as a phenomenon of ancient history—a body of literature which appeared in a certain culture, with a certain story to tell to certain ancient readers. We have seen how these readers reacted to the story, how they honored these books with canonical status, and how they handed them down to succeeding generations, until they have come into our hands. We know what the Bible was to *them;* but the crucial question is, What is it to *us?*

To some of our contemporaries its chief value consists in the information it supplies us about ancient history. They point out that the Greek historian Herodotus of the fifth century B.C., the so-called "father of history," was preceded some four hundred years by a Hebrew historian who, at that early date, wrote a brilliant account of the beginnings, growth, and final establishment of the Hebrew nation in the land of Palestine.[11] Furthermore, they note with pride the increasing respect of scholars for the historical value of his and other early narratives—a respect resulting partly from the work of archaeologists. But it may safely be said that the place which the Bible holds in the world today is emphatically not due to the quality of the history it contains. The South Sea Islanders, to whom I referred in the Preface, can hardly be considered *that* interested in history as history!

Neither is the Bible's position due primarily to its greatness as literature. And it is great literature. Charles Allen Dinsmore applied to it various literary tests and concluded that on all the tests employed it surpassed works that rate at the top of world literature—Homer's *Iliad*, Dante's *Divine Comedy*, and Shakespeare's dramas.[12] But it can

[11] This account we know as the J document. It is imbedded in the Pentateuch.

[12] *The English Bible as Literature* (Boston: Houghton Mifflin Company, 1931), pp. 3-13.

hardly be claimed that many of the world's peoples have a highly developed literary taste.

The Bible's hold on the life of the world is due to its strange and wonderful power to lead men of every race and condition into a living relationship with the God and Father of our Lord Jesus Christ. When we read it with an open mind and heart, we discover that we are not alone in an unfriendly world, victims of malevolent natural and supernatural forces which threaten to grind us and our noblest creations into dust and nothingness. We learn that God has long been seeking to enter into fellowship with us, that for centuries he spoke urgent words of invitation through the prophets whom he sent, and that at last he came to us in a Son. We discover that eternal life can begin here and now—when we forsake our foolish ways and commit ourselves, our problems, and our future to this Jesus who is called Christ. As we undertake to obey his new commandment—that we love one another—we become aware that a heavenly light begins to transfigure the dismal world in which we dwell and to shine ever more brightly until the perfect day. As we go forth in the spirit of our Lord "to preach good news to the poor," "to proclaim release to the captives," and "to set at liberty those who are oppressed," we tread on celestial ground. Life is no longer a dreary round of meaningless activity; it has been lifted to empyreal heights of magnificent adventure in company with the Creator of the universe.

Because the Bible "brings men *to* Christ, builds them up *in* Christ, and sends them out *for* Christ," the church has always claimed that it is an inspired book. The claim is fully defensible. The centuries bear witness to its redemptive role. We must not, however, claim for the Bible an authority which it does not claim for itself. It nowhere professes to be a textbook in science, sociology, philosophy, or systematic theology. In the Bible flesh-and-blood men, in their native language and idiom, bear witness to the wonderful works of God. It is a book of *testimonies* in which shepherds, fig gatherers, fishermen, and artisans pour out their souls in the dialect of the market place and the thought forms of the countryside. They do not ask us to accept their science, if indeed they had any; they want only that we should come to know their God. And when we meet him, we find that he is not a God who shackles men with the fetters of ancient thought forms but one who leads them progressively in the discovery of all truth. In the Bible we come face to face with God—and it is enough.

CHAPTER TWO

How to Understand the Bible

CLARENCE TUCKER CRAIG HAS SAID THAT THE BIBLE HAS OFTEN BEEN TREATED AS IF IT WERE "A WAX NOSE which may be twisted at the whim of the interpreter." [1] All of us have known people who could make the Bible mean whatever suited their purposes.

The axioms discussed in Chapter I lead to definite rules for interpreting the Bible. The Bible reader, like the craftsman, is limited by the character of the material with which he works. If he ignores its basic properties, his results will be worthless.

Discovering the true meaning of the words of the Bible is not a task just for scholars. Everyone who reads the Bible is faced with this responsibility. The average man naturally wants to know whether there are any rules of thumb he can follow.

Fortunately there are such rules. Throughout the history of the Christian church students of the Bible have labored diligently to formulate principles for interpreting it. Today

[1] *The Beginning of Christianity* (New York and Nashville: Abingdon-Cokesbury Press, 1943), p. 16.

there is wide agreement on a few simple rules. If these are followed, the nose cannot easily be twisted; in fact, it becomes about as inflexible as the nose of George Washington on the great stone face in the Black Hills.

RULE I: *Come to the Bible with an alert, open mind, and be ready to accept and obey whatever message the Spirit of God may impart.*

It is a sad fact that some people come to the Bible for arguments by which to substantiate their opinions and prejudices. They are like a certain ministerial recruit who, on arrival at seminary, said to a professor, "I'm not looking for any changes in my beliefs; I already have *them.* I just want arguments to support what I believe." Neither the professors nor the Holy Spirit were able to do much with that chap, as it turned out.

Neither will the Scriptures yield up their treasures to literary experts who in the moral and spiritual realms are nonchalant. It is sometimes said that no special piety is needed for interpreting the Bible, that anyone who knows the principles of literary interpretation can understand it aright. But what, we may ask, would the following verse mean to the literary critic who is a stranger to the religious reality described therein: "the kingdom of God does not mean food and drink but righteousness and peace and joy in the Holy Spirit" (Rom. 14:17)? Or again, "I have been crucified with Christ; it is no longer I who live, but Christ who lives in me; and the life I now live in the flesh I live by faith in the Son of God, who loved me and gave himself for me" (Gal. 2:20)?

Martin Luther knew well the importance of personal

religious experience in interpreting the Bible. Shortly before his death he wrote:

> No one can understand Virgil in the Bucolics and Georgics, unless for five years he has been a shepherd or a farmer. No one understands Cicero in the epistles (so I presume), unless for twenty years he has held some important office of state. No one should think that he has sufficiently tasted the holy scriptures, unless for a hundred years he has governed churches with the prophets.[2]

An important ecumenical study conference held at Oxford University in 1949 took a position in essential agreement with Luther when it concluded that "the starting point of the Christian interpreter lies within the redeemed community of which by faith he is a member." [3] The student of the Bible needs eyes that have been trained in literary disciplines, but he needs also "eyes of faith."

This does not mean, of course, that sincere non-Christians cannot read the Bible with a degree of understanding and profit. We believe that the Spirit of God will lead any honest soul in progressive comprehension of its saving message. However, it stands true that anything approaching full understanding must await both intellectual and spiritual maturity.

RULE II: *Respect the individuality of the various biblical writers.*

If, as Axiom I indicates, the Bible consists of a library of books, many of which were written by men who lived

[2] Quoted by Robert M. Grant, *The Bible in the Church* (New York: The Macmillan Co., 1948), p. 112.

[3] "Guiding Principles for the Interpretation of the Bible" in *The Bible and the Church's Message* (Geneva: Study Department of the World Council of Churches, 1949), p. 12.

in different centuries, and in some cases possibly in different millenniums, we have no right to lump the books together without regard to their individual characteristics.

The personality of each writer is stamped on his creation. He has viewed events and the world as a whole from his particular point of view: from the standpoint of his background, training, cultural environment, and religious experience. His record of historical events, if he is writing about such, will necessarily both agree with and differ from the observations of contemporary recorders who write about the same happenings. There is soul-stuff in every artistic and literary creation, and personalities come in infinite variety. We must first look through *his* eyes at what he records.

We must not, therefore, wear Pauline spectacles when we are reading Matthew's account of Jesus' ministry or Lukan spectacles when we are studying John's. If we do, we shall distort the distinctive witness of each writer and reduce the rich, many-sided testimony concerning the career of Jesus to one uninspired and uninspiring version. Neither should we explain what Jeremiah meant in a puzzling passage by what Mark meant in a less obscure one in which the same or similar words appear. Two different authors—and for that matter, the same author—may use the same word or phrase in entirely different senses.

A writer on Genesis, for example, declares that "the greater light" (the sun) and "the lesser light" (the moon) of Gen. 1:16 stand for "Christ and His people" on the ground that in Mal. 4:2 "the sun of righteousness, . . . with healing in its wings" refers to Jesus Christ and in Rev. 12:1 the moon represents Israel and the church. To import Jesus

Christ and the church into the creation story in this manner represents a considerable twist of the wax nose!

It cannot be argued that since God is the real author of the whole Bible, we have no right to look for individual differences. Jesus obviously believed that there were differences of outlook in the Old Testament. When asked if it were lawful for a man to divorce his wife, he differentiated between what Moses commanded in the Law and what, according to the creation story in Genesis, God really intended: Moses permitted divorce, but God did not want it (Mark 10:2-9). On another occasion Jesus is represented as striking a telling blow at the ceremonial legislation of the Old Testament by quoting Hos. 6:6 as an indication of God's real interest: "I desire mercy, and not sacrifice" (Matt. 9:13).

Each biblical writer has his own instrument to play in the symphony of revelation. We do them and the music no favor if we try to make them all play piccolos or bassoons.

RULE III: *Seek to determine the meaning of words at the time when they were first written and first read.*

We are all aware of the fact that the meaning of words tends to change as time passes. Since as stated in Axiom III, the Bible consists of a library of ancient books, it should be obvious that we cannot give biblical words modern meanings.

The tendency to modernize the Bible is understandable in the light of the altogether legitimate desire to apply its teachings to our modern situations. But it is nonetheless perverse. Instead of hearing the word of the Lord in the Bible, we hear the echo of our own voices.

It has been asserted, for example, that communism is

taught in the New Testament, for does not the book of Acts say, "They had everything in common" (4:32)? To read into this phrase communism of the modern variety is, of course, absurd. An examination of the stories in Acts discloses no communal production and no attempt to force a new economic pattern on society as a whole. Peter, furthermore, plainly says that Ananias was under no obligation to sell his property and give the money to the apostles (5:4). The "communism" was simply unbridled Christian generosity, a largeheartedness that touches people's bottom dollars. Because of the great need to care for the poor members of the fellowship, almost all who were able gave without stint. The contemporary propagandist, it appears, does not wish to be bothered with an investigation of the meaning of words in the time and culture in which they were written.

In the interest of clarity let us apply this rule to the interpretation of a single puzzling word in the Bible. At the hearing before the Sanhedrin, in response to the high priest's question, "Are you the Christ, the Son of the Blessed?" Jesus is reported to have answered, "I am; and you will see the Son of man sitting at the right hand of Power, and coming with the clouds of heaven" (Mark 14:62). What is meant by "Power" here? In the R.S.V. the revisers have tried to help the modern reader by capitalizing the word. They have done this because they know that in the culture in which Jesus lived it was customary, because of an acute sense of reverence for the high and holy God, to avoid use of the divine name. God was regularly referred to in some indirect way, such as the Great Glory, the Most High, Heaven, the Lord of Spirits, the Blessed, and so on. "Power," then, is a reference to God in the manner customary to Jesus' time and culture. A good modern commentary on Mark will point this out and save the reader from injecting into the term whatever may pop into his mind.

RULE IV: *Interpret words and passages in the light of their context.*

We have gone only part of the way when we have determined what a word may or may not have meant in a certain period and culture. In a given time a term may have several meanings, even when it is used by the same writer. Take our modern word "board." When we use it, we may have in mind a piece of lumber, a group of executives, the act of entering a railroad car or ship, or three meals a day. Only the context (from *con*, together, and *textus*, woven—the fabric of thought in which the word appears) can guide us in determining its meaning in a specific instance.

There are two kinds of context: the immediate and the remote. Words constitute links in a chain of words. Each chain consists of an idea. Ideas put together form paragraphs, sections, and whole books. The immediate context is the sentence in which the word belongs, the sentences immediately before and after, and the paragraph as a whole in which the word is imbedded. The remote context consists of the larger associations of the word or passage. There are degrees of remoteness, of course. The section, the book as a whole, other books written by the same author, and other literature of the same period may be said to belong to the remote context. Our task in a particular passage is to discover the direction in which the author's thought is moving and to see which of several possible meanings of a difficult word or phrase best contributes to the progress of thought. *Of all the principles of interpretation the law of the context is probably the most important.*

The significance of the context came home to me some time ago while I was listening to a sermon on the radio. The preacher was expounding with deep conviction his belief that the second coming of Christ is near. He based his remarks on Luke 17:26: "As it was in the days of Noah, so will it be in the days of the Son of man." How was it in the days of Noah? he asked. For his answer he turned to the pre-flood stories recorded in Gen. 1–5 and concluded that Noah's age was an age of city building, of polygamy, of agricultural development, of music, of metallurgy, and of violence. Comparing our time with Noah's, he affirmed that in every respect the two are strikingly similar. Since the passage declares that the Son of man will come when things are as they were in Noah's time, the conclusion that Christ is about to return seemed to him inescapable.

When he had finished, I took my New Testament and read the verse in its context. Why had he turned to Genesis for a description of Noah's time, when Jesus himself describes it (in the very next verse of Luke's Gospel)? "They ate, they drank, they married, they were given in marriage, until the day when Noah entered the ark, and the flood came and destroyed them all" (17:27). Then follows a reference to the days of Lot. People were eating, drinking, buying, selling, planting, and building when brimstone rained from heaven and exterminated them. In both references Jesus' point clearly is that destruction came swiftly, without warning, when life was going on as usual. To bring in the material from Genesis is confusing; it introduces material that Jesus did not have in mind. Furthermore, the verses just preceding the radio preacher's text likewise stress the suddenness and unpredictability of the coming of the Son of man: "The kingdom of God is not coming with the signs to be observed" (17:20); and when some say, " 'Lo, there!' or 'Lo, here!' Do not go, do not follow them. For as the lightning flashes and lights up the sky from one side to the other, so will the Son of man be in his day" (17:23-24). Nothing could be more sudden and unpredictable than lightning. Our preacher had changed the true meaning of the passage into its exact opposite. By ignoring the context he was making out of it a prediction—the very thing that Jesus said could not be done.

In the Sermon on the Mount there is a puzzling passage which is made clear when we consider the context and the way men used certain terms in that day. "The eye is the lamp of the body. So, if your eye is sound, your whole body will be full of light; but if your eye is not sound, your whole body will be full of darkness. If then the light in you is darkness, how great is the darkness!" (Matt. 6:22-23). In the King James Version the Greek words rendered here as "sound" and "not sound" appear as "single" and "evil." What is the correct translation, and what is the meaning of the passage? One of the committee members of the R.S.V., Professor Henry J. Cadbury, answers as follows:

If the terms "single eye" and "evil eye" are retained in a translation, or are rendered, as in this translation, by "sound" and "not sound," it is chiefly because nothing less than a commentary seems available to remind the reader that the eye was regarded as the seat of greed or of the reverse and that the "single eye" does not mean unity of aim but generosity and that "evil eye" does not in this context mean magic but what, using another part of the anatomy, we might designate today as tightfistedness.[4]

When the context is examined, it is seen immediately that the verses appear in the midst of a passage in which the proper attitude toward material things is being discussed. To understand the sound eye as the generous eye and the unsound one as the niggardly eye fits the context perfectly. Matthew, who introduced the verses here, certainly understood them in some such way.

In many passages the context puts content into great biblical words. The word "visit" was a favorite word of some Old Testament writers. In the contexts in which it is used it suggests that God intervenes at special moments in the course of events to work for the redemption of his people. He may come to chastise or to rescue, but his visiting is always meant to forward the ends of redemption. What "holiness" meant to Paul in I Thess. 3:13 can be determined by a careful study of chapters four and five of that letter. It involves sexual purity, brotherly love, industry, a clear understanding of Christian truth, spiritual alertness, a spirit of rejoicing and prayerfulness, etc. It is not just an emotional experience received at some particular moment, as some contemporary Christian groups seem to believe, but a quality of living.

A world-wide regard for the context, both historical and literary, would probably do more to promote a spirit of unity among the denominations and sects than any ecumenical conference the churches might hold. A sectarianism that stems from misinterpreted scripture simply cannot continue to exist where the Bible is read contextually.

[4] Luther A. Weigle and Members of the Revision Committee, *An Introduction to the Revised Standard Version of the New Testament*, p. 47.

RULE V: *Accept the simplest and most natural interpretation of a passage as its true and only meaning.*

Throughout the history of the church there have been interpreters who have insisted that the real meaning of many passages is to be found in "spiritual" or "allegorical" meanings that lie deep beneath the surface. Their search for such meanings has led to some strange interpretations. Two examples must suffice, one ancient and the other modern.

Origen, a Christian scholar of the third century, interpreted the story of Rahab in the book of Joshua in the following way: The spies represent the forerunners of Jesus, particularly John the Baptist. Rahab stands for the publicans and sinners who responded to the Baptist's message. The scarlet thread hung out the window as an identifying mark against the time of the coming invasion was a type of the saving blood of Christ. The fact that Rahab's relatives were promised safety only if they remained in her house suggests that it is only in the church that salvation through the blood of Christ is to be found.[5]

A certain recent writer finds the whole story of salvation in the first four days of creation as described in Genesis 1.[6] The earth without form and void typifies man's chaotic and sinful condition; the brooding of the Holy Spirit over the waters, the Incarnation; the firmament dividing the waters, the Cross. The latter is explained by saying that the Cross is "the great divider of mankind." It separated Jesus from God himself and from his brethren. The Resur-

[5] C. W. Dugmore, *The Interpretation of the Bible* (London: Society for Promoting Christian Knowledge, 1944), p. 18.

[6] Arthur W. Pink, *Gleanings in Genesis* (Chicago: Bible Institute Colportage Assn., 1922), I, 20 ff.

rection is said to be typified in the appearance of the dry land, and stress is laid on the fact that the dry land appeared on the third day. The Ascension is prefigured in the work of the fourth day, for on that day "our eyes are removed from the earth and all its affairs and are turned to the heavens." The writer's ingenuity is exhausted by the time he has finished the fourth day. Even with his allegorical spectacles he seems unable to discover hidden meanings in the record of days five, six, and seven. One leaves his interpretation of Gen. 1 hardly convinced that "there is much concerning Christ in this first chapter of Genesis if only we have eyes to see."

I do not mean to suggest here that the Old Testament should be interpreted without regard to the New. Without Jesus of Nazareth prophetic hopes remain unfulfilled dreams. Without the New Testament the record of God's saving activity is incomplete. Jesus Christ is indeed "the key which unlocks the golden doors into the temple of Divine truth," as the writer mentioned above so beautifully remarks.[7] More will be said about this later. But it is quite unjustifiable to foist Christian doctrine on unsuspecting and unwilling Old Testament passages. After all, they are entitled to common courtesy! When the biblical text offers a clear, straightforward meaning, we should be willing to accept it as such and not read into the record things that are not there.

In the apocalypses (Daniel and Revelation) we are of course obliged to look for deeper meanings. Here meanings were deliberately concealed under the cloak of symbolic language. As explained in the previous chapter, apocalypses

[7] *Ibid.*, p. 20.

were underground writings. Their aim was to keep alive in the hearts of the persecuted the hope of eventual liberation. They counseled resistance to the demands of the tyrannical overlords and predicted their destruction by God in the not distant future. It is reported that books of this kind circulated in the underground during the period of Nazi domination of Europe. It is understandable why one must look deeper than the surface for meanings in such literature. In reading the biblical apocalypses you will need to seek help in commentaries written by responsible scholars.

Martin Luther stated long ago in a clear and forceful way the principle of interpretation with which we are concerned here. He said:

> No violence is to be done to the words of God, whether by man or angel; but they are to be retained in their simplest meaning wherever possible, and to be understood in their grammatical and literal sense unless the context plainly forbids, lest we give our adversaries occasion to make a mockery of all the scriptures.[8]

RULE VI: *Interpret passages in the light of their basic literary character.*

In the discussion of Axiom I it was pointed out that the Bible contains many types of literature. Due regard for the basic nature of each type must be had if its true meaning is to be gained.

The necessity of special care in interpreting the apocalyptic material has already been urged.

Letters must be considered in the light of the circumstances of the writers and of the original readers. They

[8] Quoted by Robert M. Grant, *op. cit.*, p. 117.

must not be regarded as primarily teaching general truths, universally applicable, but as offering practical counsels for the benefit of specific readers in specific situations. The instructions given in them may or may not be relevant in other situations and other times.

It is now widely recognized that the Gospels are not biographies or works of history, but rather testimonials by their writers to their faith in Jesus as Saviour and Lord. As testimonials they were meant to edify Christians in faith and life and to convince interested inquirers of the truth of the claims made about Jesus. They are thus propaganda literature (in a good sense). We must not, then, expect to find in them pure history, but rather interpreted history; and we must not criticize them unjustly for not offering us the kind of information historians are accustomed to give.

The aphorisms of the book of Proverbs are salty, incisive utterances of truths to which the wise person will give heed. They appear in several literary forms. The simplest consists of a single line of Hebrew poetry divided into two equal parts. In an English translation the parts are properly printed as couplets. Groupings of several lines are also found, each grouping constituting a closely knit unit. In interpreting these longer or shorter units the context will be of little—and often of no—importance. Couplets without logical arrangement appear in Prov. 10:1–22:16, while longer units in more or less systematic arrangement are to be found in Prov. 1–9. It is obvious that proverbs cannot be treated as one would treat a running narrative.

It is recognized by all scholars today that much of the Old Testament is poetic in nature. When the King James Version was published, the characteristics of Hebrew poetry were not known; hence, even the Psalms were printed in exactly the same form as the historical record in the books of Samuel. Since 1753, when Bishop Lowth set forth his now famous conclusions on the basic features of Hebrew poetry, scholars have been adding to his findings and identifying more and more of the poetry of the Bible. Hebrew poetry has rhythm but ordinarily not rhyme. Its most characteristic feature is "parallelism of members," "rhyming of thoughts." The second line of a couplet (a couplet is the simplest unit of Hebrew verse) may repeat the thought of the first line in varying words, may present a contrasting thought, or may complete the idea begun in the first line. Several lines may be built together in a definite, logical structure of thought. A degree of rhythmic regularity and systematic structure of the thought are thus characteristic marks of Hebrew poetry.[9]

In the R.S.V. 40 per cent of the Old Testament is printed as poetry.[10] The chief poetic parts are the Psalms, Job, Proverbs, the Song of Solomon, Lamentations, and much of the various prophetic books. Scattered through the prose narrative contained in the Pentateuch and the books of Joshua, Judges, Samuel, and Kings are poetic pieces of varying dates and excellence. In Genesis we have such pieces as Adam's naming of Eve (2:23), the cursing of the serpent, Eve, and Adam (3:14-19), the song of Lamech (4:23-24), the curse and blessings uttered by Noah (9:25-27), Melchizedek's blessing of Abram (14:19-20), God's words to Rebekah concerning her unborn children (25:23), Isaac's blessing of Jacob (27:27-29) and of Esau (27:39-40),

[9] See A.B.C., pp. 154-57.

[10] Weigle (*et al.*), *An Introduction to the Revised Standard Version of the Old Testament*, p. 63.

Jacob's blessing of Ephraim and Manasseh (48:15-16, 20), and his blessing of his sons (49: 2-27). In Exodus we find the songs of Moses and Miriam (15:1-18, 21), in Numbers the Aaronic blessing (6:24-26) and the ancient song of the well (21:17-18), and so on. So poetic in quality is the prose narrative of Genesis that scholars consider it likely that many of its stories were sung in verse by minstrels before they were reduced to prose by early writers.

It will come as a surprise to some of you to learn that the prophets cast their fiery proclamations in poetic form. To many Americans poetry seems artificial and even effeminate. But in ancient times no such reaction prevailed. Primitive passions burst forth in the rhythmic chant of battle songs. By their wild notes the tribes were summoned to the fray and victorious warriors welcomed home. Biting satire, as in the taunt-song over fallen Moab (Num. 21:27-30), fell from exultant lips in poetic form. When the prophets used the traditional cadences, they were speaking in the strongest medium available to them. High emotion and great ideas can be conveyed in poetry more adequately than in pedestrian prose. And what is said in poetry will be remembered longer.

It is now known that Jesus occasionally clothed his message in poetic dress. The basic features of Hebrew poetry are exhibited in such sayings as

> He makes his sun rise on the evil and on the good,
> And sends rain on the just and on the unjust.
> —Matt. 5:45

Here the second line repeats the thought of the first. In other sayings the second line presents a contrasting idea:

Every sound tree bears good fruit,
But the bad tree bears evil fruit.[11]
—Matt. 7:17

Jesus used many forms in his teaching, but when he used the poetic, he was following in the goodly tradition set by Israel's bards, prophets, and wise men.

It is a commonplace that one must approach poetry in a different frame of mind from prose. Prose is matter-of-fact; it is meant to be taken more or less literally. Poetry is highly imaginative. It abounds in metaphors. By them it suggests more than it says. It is designed to arouse deep emotion, not to teach cold facts. When the sacred writer says (Isa. 55:12),

The mountains and the hills before you
shall break forth into singing,
and all the trees of the field shall clap their hands,

he obviously does not intend for us to take him literally.

If you will take pains to discover the spirit and literary form of the material you are reading and let your interpretation be governed by them, you will not go far wrong.

RULE VII: *View each part of the Bible in the light of the whole Bible.*

It was stated in Axiom II that the Bible consists of a library of related books, for almost without exception they are concerned directly or indirectly with God's redemptive activity in behalf of men. It was also pointed out that the

[11] For other examples see C. F. Burney, *The Poetry of Our Lord* (Oxford: Clarendon Press, 1925).

New Testament claims that this redemptive activity became fully effective in Jesus of Nazareth.

Is the New Testament claim true? Was God preparing the way for Jesus' coming? Do the Law, the Prophets, and the Psalms point to him, as asserted in Luke 24:27, 44? Is Paul justified in holding that the Jews cannot understand their Scriptures until they turn to Jesus Christ (II Cor. 3:14-16)? Is he the fulfiller of the Law and the Prophets (Matt. 5:17)? Do the yearnings of the worthies of the Old Testament for a more perfect relationship between God and his people find their realization in the blessed community brought into being by Jesus? Is the blameless life, which the psalmist (Ps. 15:1-2) affirmed as a requisite for dwelling on God's holy hill, really possible for him who puts his faith in Jesus Christ? To answer yes requires an affirmation of faith—a confession based on experience. This affirmation and confession Christians of all ages have unhesitatingly made. It has not seemed incredible that God's word, so long spoken to the prophets, should at last become incarnate in a Son, the man Christ Jesus.

If it is true that Jesus becomes to all who obey him "the source of eternal salvation" (Heb. 5:9) and is therefore to be seen as the focal personage in all the Bible, certain consequences for interpretation follow.

1. God's *full* will for men is disclosed in the person, deeds, and words of Jesus, not in the laws, ceremonies, and ethics of the Old Testament. Since the Old Testament comes out of an earlier and preparatory stage in God's self-disclosure, everything in it must be measured by the yardstick given us in Jesus Christ. Whatever actions, attitudes, and injunctions in it do not measure up to Jesus' new com-

mandment—that we love one another, including our enemies—must be labeled sub-Christian and therefore not normative for us. This does not mean that we shall despise the Old Testament. We shall thank God most heartily for the valiant men of old who, peering through the fog of idolatry and barbarism in which they and their fellows were enveloped, yet caught glimpses of "the city which has foundations, whose builder and maker is God" and pressed toward it. We shall not censure them for their faulty vision but only rejoice that for us the mists have been rolled away.

2. Though we shall not import Jesus into passages of the Old Testament, as has been done by both ancient and modern interpreters, we shall be alert to recognize those places where the full meaning can be discerned only from the vantage point of the revelation in him.

With respect to the New Covenant it will not be hard to see that Jeremiah and Jesus represent promise and fulfillment. The utterances of neither can be understood without the words of the other (Jer. 31:31-34; Mark 14:24; I Cor. 11:25).

That Jesus interpreted his ministry in the light of Isa. 53 seems almost beyond dispute. It is not necessary to hold that the prophet looked forward to the coming of the man Jesus when he wrote this amazing chapter; it may well be that he had the suffering, righteous remnant of Israel in mind.[12] He believed that this remnant would somehow by its suffering win the whole of Israel, yea, even the Gentiles, to the worship and service of "the Creator of the ends of the earth." The Christian sees that in the providence of God this was accomplished through the sufferings of Jesus of

[12] See, for example, Isa. 44:1, 21; 45:4; 49:3, 5-7.

Nazareth and the sacrificial obedience of his followers. The prophecies of Isaiah were thus fulfilled, as the early Christians clearly saw.

If one recognizes that the book of Genesis cannot be understood fully apart from the Gospels and the book of Revelation, one does not thereby fall into the pit of allegorical interpretation along with Origen.[13] In Genesis the God who created men for righteous fellowship with himself, only to find this fellowship soon broken by man's willfulness, is represented as beginning the search for his wayward children that he may restore them to their rightful place. Much of the Old Testament is the record of his redemptive activity in the life and work of Israel's leaders and prophets. The New Testament depicts his saving activity in Jesus of Nazareth and his obedient followers. The latter, by their wholehearted response to God, to his Son and Servant, and to one another, soon found that they were members of a blessed community in which the lost fellowship had been regained. The book of Revelation looks forward to the time when this community will embrace "every tribe and tongue and people and nation" (Rev. 5:9), when all the redeemed will stand in God's very presence in intimate, holy fellowship and do his will forevermore. Genesis is incomplete without Revelation, and Revelation is inexplicable without Genesis.

A word about the use of the rules presented in this chapter should be offered. Some are more important than others. Some appear on the surface to be contradictory. Experience alone can show when this one or that should be applied to the passage under consideration. Interpreting

[13] See p. 41.

the Bible is somewhat like interpreting a musical score. One must know not only the mechanics of music as represented by the score but also how in utilizing them to transcend them in the creation of tonal, rhythmic, and dramatic effects. The beginner must of necessity content himself for the moment with something less than an "inspired" interpretation.

CHAPTER THREE

Reading a Book as a Whole

THE PERSON WHO IS LOOKING FOR A WAY TO MASTER THE BIBLE "IN THREE EASY LESSONS" WILL BE DISAPPOINTED in this guide for reading it. In the first place one can never "master" the Bible; one can only be mastered by it. In the second place the Bible is so incalculably rich that the human mind cannot possibly embrace it all in a few attempts at understanding.

Familiarity with the Bible comes by long exposure of the personality to its contents in the proper reading situation. In some respects coming to know the Bible is like getting acquainted with a neighbor. A rewarding friendship hardly results from a "hello" when two neighbors are passing on the street or an exchange of words when one is borrowing a wheelbarrow. The neighbors must play golf together, "root" together for the local baseball team, argue with each other over politics and the social system, ring doorbells together for the community chest—in short, expose their whole personalities to each other in sustained relationships.

It is my fervent hope, however, that the reading of this book will make it very much easier for you to come to know the Bible in an intimate way. There are to be found here definite principles and procedures which, if followed, will bring you speedily into the holy of holies of biblical truth. But you will need to tarry there until your eyes and lungs become accustomed to the dazzling light and celestial atmosphere. You cannot rush in and out and come to know the majestic One who dwells there.

Sound methods of reading the Bible make use of all one's capacities: mind, will, emotions. It is not enough to learn how to get a "spiritual lift" out of reading, for this will leave the mind and will unemployed. On the other hand, exclusive attention to intellectual or volitional concerns will be quite as unsatisfying. Too few people bring to the Bible their whole personalities. The literary man brings his mind and emotions but reserves his will. The religious legalist offers his will in the attempt to obey biblical commands but holds back his mind and emotions. The fundamentalist gladly surrenders his will and emotions but denies that he has any right to use his mind in testing and questioning the biblical revelation. But here, as elesewhere, God wants the whole man.

Those of you who are accustomed only to devotional reading of the Bible may become impatient with the academic flavor of the reading procedures to be set forth in this book. It should be obvious, however, that we cannot vow allegiance to the truth contained in the Bible and joyfully and enthusiastically follow it out in daily living until we understand it *with our minds*. God's word to us is expressed in the thought of the writers of the various biblical books. If we misunderstand their thought, we may devote our energies to unworthy ends. Since this thought is expressed in literary forms, nothing can take the place of knowledge and use of accepted methods of literary interpretation. By sympathetic and prayerful application of these methods, food for the soul as well as for the mind will result.

If our reading of the Bible is to result in growth of understanding as well as in moral obedience and healthy emotional response, we must have regard for the laws of learning as we approach the Bible. Fundamental in learning is the principle of logical coherence. Unrelated ideas are about as odious to the mind as splinters to the cell structure of a finger. But ideas which are related in some pattern of thought bring pleasurable and profitable experience.

Not all books of the Bible follow through logically from beginning to end. These are not therefore fundamentally unified (one). Scholars of today know that some are like great snowballs which, as they rolled down through the centuries following their first appearance in written form, gathered up materials of various types. They are aggregations of literary pieces rather than compositions. Such a book is Jeremiah. It is obvious that a book of this type cannot be read as one would read a composition by one author, in which the material follows in logical sequence from beginning to end.[1]

For the purposes of reading we shall divide the books of the Bible into two classes: unified or substantially unified

[1] Whether a book had one or several authors is not, however, the decisive consideration in determining how it should be read. Second Corinthians appears to consist of fragments of three letters, all written by the same author (Paul); but the book is not thereby unified. It is quite possible for several writers to contribute to a book in such a way that the final result holds together structurally and logically. The important consideration for reading is whether there is satisfactory coherence of thought in the book *as it now lies before us.*

books, and nonunified books. The former can be read as wholes; the latter must be read piece by piece, often in an order different from that in which the pieces now lie in the various books.

Competent biblical scholars do not entirely agree in their conclusions concerning the unity of biblical books. The matter is very complicated. In certain instances only tentative judgments are possible. The following rough classification will serve as a working basis for our program of reading:

Unified or Substantially Unified Books

Old Testament

Genesis, Exodus, Numbers, Deuteronomy, Joshua, Judges, Ruth, First and Second Samuel, First and Second Kings, First and Second Chronicles, Ezra, Nehemiah, Esther, Daniel, Jonah

New Testament

Matthew, Mark, Luke, John, Acts, Romans, First Corinthians, Galatians, Ephesians, Philippians, Colossians, First and Second Thessalonians, First and Second Timothy, Titus, Philemon, Hebrews, First and Second Peter, First, Second, and Third John, Jude, Revelation

Nonunified Books

Old Testament

Leviticus, Job, Psalms, Proverbs, Ecclesiastes, Song of Solomon, Isaiah, Jeremiah, Lamentations, Ezekiel, Hosea, Joel, Amos, Obadiah, Micah, Nahum, Habakkuk, Zephaniah, Haggai, Zechariah, Malachi

New Testament

Second Corinthians, James

Before turning to specific instructions for reading the unified or substantially unified books, I should like to comment briefly on two introductory suggestions.

The first is, *Set apart a period at regular intervals for reading the Bible by yourself*. It is doubtful whether "catch-as-catch-can" reading is worth even the snatches of time given to it. Harried Christians who demand of the Bible that it yield up its treasures in two minutes flat are likely to come away with empty hands. When the reading is carried on according to a plan, one comes to the appointed hour in a spirit of quiet confidence and expectancy. "The attitude of Bible-reading," says Alan Richardson, "is rather that of a lover waiting at the trysting-place than that of a general storming a citadel." [2] By reading alone one avoids the distractions that inevitably accompany the presence of another, no matter how near and dear. Professor Paul S. Minear has said eloquently what ought to be said here: "Read when you are alone, when you have time to think seriously about yourself, when you want to understand your own life and death, when you reflect about the source and goal of that inner center which you call yourself." [3]

Secondly, *Get yourself equipped at the outset with the materials needed for effective reading*. Ideally these should include a copy of the R.S.V., a concordance, a Bible dictionary, an atlas of the lands of the Bible, a good one-volume commentary on the whole Bible, a notebook, and pen and ink.[4] Probably not many of you will be able to obtain all

[2] *Preface to Bible Study* (Philadelphia: The Westminster Press, 1944), p. 17.

[3] *A Preface to the New Testament* (privately published), p. 2.

[4] Suggestions concerning the selection of books will be found on pp. 147-50. There is at present no concordance to the R.S.V. In due time one will be available. Readers should watch for announcements of its appearance.

these tools. But by all means secure, in addition to the R.S.V., *The Abingdon Bible Commentary* (or one of the other standard one-volume commentaries) and suitable writing materials. You are to embark on one of the most important undertakings of life, and you must be adequately equipped.

Now, how shall one set about to read the unified or substantially unified books?

I. *Concentrate on a book at a time.*

Reading verses at random—wherever the Bible happens to open–is about like ducking for apples blindfolded. Who would think of reading a paragraph one day from Douglas' *The Robe*, half a dozen sentences the second day from Eisenhower's *Crusade in Europe*, and a similar amount the third day from Steinbeck's *The Grapes of Wrath?* It is only common courtesy to hear an author through to the end of his book in something approaching a connected fashion, so that the lines of thought are kept clearly in mind. It is a tribute to the richness of the Bible that anything at all can be gained from desultory reading. The best approach is certainly to concentrate on a book at a time, until you are on speaking terms with its author.

II. *Survey the whole book before beginning detailed study of the parts.*

Individual books of the Bible have no table of contents or preface by which one can get an idea of the whole. This can be accomplished only by rapid reading or scanning. Someone has said that the proper order is first the telescope and then the microscope.

Getting acquainted with a biblical book is something like becoming familiar with the landscape of unknown territory. One must somehow get above the woods and the towering hills to a place where the whole countryside can be seen at a glance. From this high point one sees how the mountains and valleys, the rivers and cities, the waste lands and the cultivated areas, relate to one another. When the layout of the terrain as a whole has been grasped, the segments that comprise the whole can be explored pleasurably and understandingly.

According to Julian Price Love "more than half of the sixty-six books can be read in an average of about twenty minutes, no one of them requiring an hour." [5] The importance of this method of reading came to him one day in college when he read Paul's letter to the Galatians through in fifteen minutes. Says he of this college student's unforgettable experience, "The thrill that came over him drew him into the ardor of the apostle so potently that the glow has never died." [6] James Stalker, a well-known Scottish scholar of half a century ago, in his student days had a similar experience with the Epistle to the Romans and resolved thereafter that he would always read biblical books through at a sitting before taking up detailed study of the parts.[7]

A. The First Reading of the Whole

When you have put yourself in an attitude of alert receptivity, proceed *at one sitting* to read rapidly or scan the

[5] *How to Read the Bible* (New York: The Macmillan Co., 1940), p. 16.

[6] *Ibid.*, p. 23.

[7] James M. Gray, *How to Master the English Bible* (Chicago: Winona Publishing Co., 1904), p. 19.

book selected. What is wanted is a total impression. Your purpose is to see what the book as a whole will do to you. A book will do various things to various people, and the same book at another time will speak a fresh, and in some respects a different, word to the same person.

The experience involved in this first reading is comparable to the impression one receives on walking into the presence of a great work of art for the first time, say Michelangelo's *Last Judgment*. The beholder is at first overpowered by the sheer immensity of this sixty-six by thirty-three foot painting covering a whole wall of the Sistine Chapel. Then comes a feeling of confusion. The scores of huge, muscular, contorted human figures, tumbling over one another, many with anguished countenances; the sea of faces peering out of the black background; the splashes of light illuminating the eerie scene; the variety and profusion of objects carried in the hands and strewn about—all plunge the viewer into near panic. But as one gazes, the confusion begins to melt away. It is seen that the painting is a religious painting, for crosses, angels, and a crown of thorns appear. The eye slowly but surely makes its way to the gesturing, half-crouching central figure, Christ the Judge, toward whom many are turned eagerly and expectantly and from whom others are running away in terror. The hundreds of intertwined legs at length become connected with their torsos, and the figures are seen to fall into definite groupings set off from one another by spaces stretching across the painting. The Virgin Mary, saints, martyrs, angels, demons, the damned—all appear in some understandable relationship to the central figure, Christ the Judge. Though puzzling features remain and send one scurrying through his guidebook for explanations, the initial confusion has turned into a large degree of clarity as one has simply *looked*.

On first contact the profusion of words and ideas in a biblical book probably will bewilder you. However, if you will continue reading to the end, with your mind wide awake, the chances are that you will discover some sort of unity underlying the verbiage and grasp something of the plan of the book. The effectiveness of the reading will be increased by keeping in mind five questions. Jottings should be made in your notebook in answer to these questions.

1. *What kind of book is this?* Is it prose or poetry, or are the two mixed so that it might appropriately be called poetic prose? If it is prose, can it be characterized more closely? Is it historical narrative, legal matter, short story, sermonic material, personal correspondence, or vision and revelation (apocalypse)? If it is poetry, is it lyric poetry (like the Psalms), dramatic poetry (like Job), elegy (like Lamentations), wise sayings (like Proverbs), or prophetic oracles (like the words of Jeremiah)? If the types are mixed, in what proportions do the various types appear? It will be recalled that the precise use of the rules of interpretation discussed in Chapter II depends on the character of the materials to be interpreted. One must not, for example, interpret historical narrative, poetry, and apocalypse in exactly the same way. If you are not certain of the exact type, do not be overly concerned; you will pick up this information from some of your collateral reading at a later stage.

2. *What gives the book its unity?* Is the unifying factor a person, a group of persons, a problem, an idea, an event of the past, present, or future, or what? Attempt to state

this unity in a sentence, or at most in a short paragraph.

As an illustration of what is meant by the two questions above, let us consider the book of Deuteronomy. A survey of this book would lead one to conclude that it consists of sermonic (chapters 1–11; 27–31), legal (chapters 12–26), poetic (chapters 32–33), and historical (chapter 34) materials. The sermonic greatly preponderates; even the legal material is represented as part of the sermons preached by Moses. The unity of the book might be stated somewhat as follows: Shortly before his death Moses exhorted the people of Israel, who were about to enter the land of Canaan, to remember the laws given to their fathers at the holy mountain and to obey them after arriving in the Promised Land. He reviewed these laws for their benefit, pointed out the consequences of obedience and disobedience, and gave them his parting blessing.

Scholars of today know that several writers contributed parts of the book of Deuteronomy over a period of nearly two hundred years, but since their contributions were made in the spirit of the original book, the whole is substantially unified.

Further study of a book will undoubtedly reveal limitations in the statement of unity you will draw up at this point, but a beginning will have been made.

3. *What structural features does the book contain?* Is it a house with many rooms of equal size and character? Are some large and some small in line with their varying functions? Or has it a simple, one-room plan?

Modern books have a table of contents in which the author's outline is clearly visible. Frequently the subject is divided into parts, the parts into chapters, and the chapters into sections. The mind of the reader is thus able to move from point to point with a clear sense of direction. Biblical writers were not as careful to be strictly logical in their writing or to inform their readers of the structure of their creations. They left more responsibility to the inquiring mind. But their books on the whole are not thrown together haphazardly, though at first contact they may seem to be. The power they have exerted over the minds of men through the centuries testifies to the fact that these books are basically understandable.

In the R.S.V. the revisers have attempted to help the reader by careful paragraphing of the material throughout and by sometimes introducing spaces in the text at points in a book where the thought logically divides.[8] The large divisions thus produced constitute the "rooms" of the "house." It is left to the reader to write in his own captions, to inscribe "kitchen," "dining room," and "bedroom" over the various doorways. In some modern translations and editions of the Bible, such as the Old Testament portion of *The Complete Bible–An American Translation* and *The Westminster Study Edition of the Holy Bible*, the editors have attempted to help the reader understand the relationship of the parts to the whole by the use of captions. There is a danger in this, for readers are apt to get the idea that the captions are part of the original biblical text, rather than the work of modern editors. Furthermore, in the very nature of the case there can be no authoritative analysis and characterization of the text. Equally good minds will

[8] The introduction of spacing to mark thought divisions has not been done with equal care throughout the R.S.V. In the Old Testament it is used in the poetic, but rarely in the prose, materials. More of it appears in the New Testament. It is to be hoped that in future editions the editors will pay more attention to this sound and helpful way of assisting the reader.

come away from the same passage with somewhat different results. It is better to leave the outlining to the individual reader. As he grapples with the thought development himself, his mind and spirit will grow.

If the structure of the book is not clear on this first reading, a second reading, to be described below, will probably make it plain.

4. *What reaction does the book stimulate in me?* Does it inspire, convict, entertain, puzzle, or bore me? Exactly why do I feel this way? First impressions may not be sound impressions, but they should be recorded in your notebook anyhow. Further study may confirm or dissipate them.

5. *What features of the contents are puzzling?* It will be best at this point simply to list them. At a later point in the reading process the answers may be obvious. You are not ready to tackle them now.

When the first reading has been completed, you will have formed a judgment about the book. You will know whether you want to keep on with it or move on to a more rewarding portion of the Bible. Books are like people: some intrigue and some fatigue. Later on, after many biblical books have become familiar friends, you may find that those passed up earlier are not quite so boring as they at first seemed to be. The longer one reads the Bible, the less he finds himself judging it, and the more he discovers himself being judged by it.

B. The Second Reading of the Whole

If you have decided to continue with the book selected, a second rapid reading—or scanning if it is long—should be undertaken. In this reading you should gather specific data on various matters of importance. Results should be recorded in your notebook.

1. *Circumstances connected with the writing of the book should be carefully noted.* The importance of seeing the book against its historical background was stressed in the discussion of Axiom III in Chapter I and Rule III in Chapter II.

Who was the author, and what were his circumstances at the time of writing? Is there a direct claim concerning the authorship anywhere in the text, apart from the title? The titles appearing in the English versions were not part of the original manuscripts. Hebrew books were known by their opening words. Genesis, for example, was called "In the beginning." The English titles of Old Testament books are derived from the Greek translation of the Old Testament (the Septuagint) by way of the Latin version (the Vulgate). The titles of New Testament books were all assigned by the early church and represent the tradition concerning their authorship current in the first centuries. The tradition may be sound, or it may be unsound. The text of the book needs to be checked to see whether the assigned authorship can seriously be maintained. Though the value of a book is not dependent on the identity of its author, our understanding of it will obviously be enhanced if we know who wrote it.

When and where the various books were written are facts often hard to come by. Biblical writers did not date their books as we do today, nor were they careful to indicate their whereabouts. A book cannot, of course, be earlier than the latest event mentioned in it. The book of Genesis, at least in its present form, cannot be earlier than the time of the foundation of the Hebrew monarchy shortly before

1000 B.C., on the evidence of Gen. 36:31: "These are the kings who reigned in the land of Edom, before any king reigned over the Israelites." How much later than this must be decided on the basis of many clues. The book of Acts cannot have been written prior to Paul's imprisonment in Rome, for the book ends with the record of that imprisonment. Few problems in biblical studies are fraught with so much difficulty as that concerning the exact dating of the various books. Scholars have to fall back on such inconclusive data as the kind of language used, the character of the subject matter, references to historical events and to other books mentioned in the text, and the like. In letters the place and circumstances of the writer will obviously be more important than in a historical work. If after two readings clear evidence is still lacking, a standard reference book should be consulted.

What information about the identity and circumstances of its first readers can be gained from the book? It was emphasized under Axiom III that, almost without exception, the books of the Bible had immediate, practical purposes when they were written. Of fundamental importance is the discovery of these purposes. Every allusion to the readers and their condition should be noted. In addition one often can infer from the subjects discussed and the nature of the instruction given what the author's purpose in writing was.

2. *The writer's characteristic words, phrases, and ideas should be listed.* Every person's style of speaking and writing is indelibly marked by qualities of his personality. If favorite words and expressions are prominent and peculiar, we call them mannerisms. They tell us much about the writer's mind. Often-repeated words and phrases also give

one a clue to his special emphases. Matthew's characteristic expressions ("the kingdom of heaven," "men will weep and gnash their teeth," "righteousness," "that it might be fulfilled," "hypocrites," "the law and the prophets") convey central emphases in his portrait of Jesus. Repeated words and phrases may also afford a clue to the book's structure. Matthew's standard formula of transition from one section to another is, "And when Jesus had finished . . ." (7:28; 11:1; 13:53; 19:1; 26:1). This formula marks the transition from discourse to narrative and, apart from the introduction and conclusion, divides the book into five major sections, each with a narrative introduction and a concluding discourse. It seems that Matthew has deliberately organized his book after the pattern of the Pentateuch, for he wishes to set Jesus forth as the Second Moses, who has given a new and higher law.

One can also determine the author's special interests by the type of material he includes and excludes. Luke, for example, introduces a great deal of material about the prayer life of Jesus and the early church, the Holy Spirit, and the social implications of the gospel. He leaves out sayings of Jesus (like those recorded in Matt. 10:5; 15:24) which seem to limit Jesus' interest and work to Jews, for he wishes to represent Jesus as the universal Saviour. The author of the Fourth Gospel was interested in the inner consciousness of Jesus far more than were the writers of the Synoptic Gospels; this conclusion is easily reached when one observes the content of the discourses of Jesus presented in his book in comparison with those of the Synoptics.

3. *Emotional qualities of the book should be discerned.* The power of a literary work over men's minds is due in

no small degree to these qualities. Luke's beautiful story of the life and teaching of Jesus is moving not only because of his subject but also because of his artistry in telling the story. He has a flair for the dramatic. He introduces the elements of suspense and pathos frequently. There is a marked note of joy in Luke-Acts, beginning with the very first chapters. The words "praising God," "glorified God," "rejoice," and "joy" occur over and over. God in his graciousness has come to men with salvation, and what he has done has set the heavens and the earth to singing.

4. *The plan of the book is of fundamental importance.* It was suggested that attention be given to this on the first reading. Because many of the books of the Bible are complex structures, it may take some living with a particular book to discover its plan. The ideal interpreter has X-ray eyes. He can look beneath the flesh to the skeleton. Dissection for the purpose of study can thus be made at the joints. The beginner must not be discouraged by his inadequate initial attempts. He will grow in his ability to analyze material if he keeps at it.

The clues to structure are many and various. It was pointed out in describing the first reading that in the R.S.V. the revisers may have assisted you by the use of spaces at the end of logical sections. For example, First Corinthians has been divided as follows: 1:1-3; 1:4–4:21; 5:1–6:20; 7:1-40; 8:1-13; 9:1-27; 10:1–11:1; 11:2-34; 12:1–14:40; 15:1-58; 16:1-20; 16:21-24. If no spacing appears in the book to indicate the units, you will have to go it on your own, taking advantage of such clues to structure as there are.

The writer may have stated his plan at some point in his book. In the book of Acts the outline is clearly suggested in 1:8. The disciples are to witness "in Jerusalem and in all Judea and Samaria, and to the end of the earth." Witnessing in Jerusalem is described in 1:1–8:3, in Judea and Samaria in 8:4–12:25, and to the end of the earth in chapters 13–28. Similarly, the plan of the book of Revelation is indicated in 1:19: "what you see" (in the vision of the heavenly Son of man) is described in chapter 1; "what is" (the conditions in the churches) is set forth in chapters 2 and 3; and "what is to take place hereafter" (the steps in the consummation of all things) is detailed in chapters 4–22.

Usually the plan is not stated, and the reader must discover it. A major shift in the character of the subject matter will often mark a division point. For example, a reading of the book of Joshua will reveal the fact that the narrative moves through three stages: the story of the conquest of Canaan (chapters 1–12); an account of the allotment of territory in the land to the various participating tribes (chapters 13–21); and a concluding portion setting forth the final deeds and words of Joshua (chapters 22–24).

Sometimes a book is built up on the geographical principle. The Gospel of Mark, after the introduction (1:1-13), may be outlined as follows: Jesus' ministry in Galilee (1:14–7:23); his withdrawal to the regions north of Galilee and his return to Capernaum (7:24–9:50); the journey to and crisis in Jerusalem (10:1–16:8).

The reader's task is to find the principle on which the book is put together. When he understands both the book's unity and its diversity, he has taken a long step in the mastery of the whole. Let it be repeated that ability to analyze literary material grows with practice. The sooner one begins it, the better.

5. *The purpose and message of the book should now be summarized.* In a sense this is an overview of the overview. The two readings have resulted in the accumulation of many significant data concerning the writer, the readers and their circumstances, and the outstanding features of the book. Go over these data and draw up a brief statement that expresses exactly why the book was written—what the author wanted to say to his readers. It is helpful to select a statement from the book itself which seems to epitomize the writer's message. This will not be possible in all cases, but it is worth while when it can be done.

C. Checking on Your Results

You have now, as it were, surveyed the landscape from a high hill. You have seen much with your own two eyes. But have you observed accurately? Perhaps a shimmering ribbon in the distance, which you took to be a river, is a long bank of snow. Perhaps the range of mountains on the horizon really consists of two parallel ranges with a valley between. It is important that you identify correctly the major features of the terrain before you undertake detailed exploration, lest time and strength be lost.

At such a time an experienced explorer, who knows every foot of the ground, can offer invaluable help. You are ready now to ask him questions, the kind of questions you could not possibly have formulated had you not first looked with your own eyes. Of course, you might have stayed at the bottom of the hill and besought him, from his expert knowledge, to draw a map for you. But you would have missed the thrill of exploration, the soul-stretching experience of seeing and appreciating for yourself. Your knowledge would always have been secondhand.

You should now turn to a good reference book. A.B.C. has introductions to the various biblical books in which authorship, date, readers and their situation, literary features, purpose of the book, and other matters are considered. A more detailed discussion of these and related points will be found in the introductions to the Old and New Testaments, listed on pages 149-50. Here are the experienced explorers. Don't be afraid to argue with them. They obviously know more than you do, but their knowledge is not infallible. In the interpretation and evaluation of data experts frequently disagree. You are entitled to your say, to the extent, of course, that you can back it up with good evidence. The double process of checking on the experts and letting them check on you will result in rapid growth in understanding.

If time permits, go over each of the points you have covered. At the very least consider carefully what the scholars say about the kind of book it is, the identity of the author and the first readers, the circumstances of both, the plan of the book, and its purpose. These points are basic prerequisites for proceeding with the next major step in the reading process.

CHAPTER FOUR

Examining the Parts and Re-viewing the Whole

IT WAS SUGGESTED IN THE PREVIOUS CHAPTER THAT UNIFIED BOOKS ARE LIKE HOUSES. SOME ARE COMPLEX STRUCTURES consisting of several wings with rooms of many sizes and uses, and some are little more than one-room cottages.[1] One of the major purposes of the initial survey, it was stated, is to gain a knowledge of the general layout, so that systematic, detailed examination can be undertaken.

It is assumed by most readers of the King James Version that the chapters of each book constitute the "rooms" of the "house." Unfortunately, this is not always the case. In the original manuscripts there were no chapter or verse divisions. The former were made by Stephen Langton in the thirteenth century and the latter by Robert Stephanus in the sixteenth. It does not take much discernment to conclude that in many places the divisions were not skillfully

[1] I am indebted to Mortimer J. Adler, *How to Read a Book* (New York: Simon & Schuster, Inc., 1940), p. 163, for this metaphor and for some highly rewarding insights concerning methods of reading.

made. When thought units are broken up by verse and chapter divisions, the reader can hardly be blamed for failing to grasp the writer's meaning. In the R.S.V. the revisers have given careful attention to units of thought. They have printed the material in paragraphs, sometimes overriding the chapter divisions;[2] and they have at many places introduced spaces into the text to indicate major division points.[3]

It may be helpful to pursue the house metaphor further. Words are the bricks from which the house is constructed. Words put together in sentences are like bricks cemented together in layers. The resultant wall, say of a bedroom, may be compared with the paragraph. Several interrelated walls comprise a room (a section or chapter). A group of rooms constitute a wing of the house (the major divisions of a book), and the wings together make up the whole house (the book as a unit). When one is studying houses, the place to begin is hardly with individual bricks, layers of bricks, or walls. It only makes sense to begin with the general layout.

The plan of a house is determined by several considerations: the size of the family or families to occupy it, the biological and social needs of the individual residents, cost and availability of materials, prevailing styles of architecture, and the preferences of the architect or the future inhabitants. A house bears unmistakable marks of the period and culture out of which it came. So it is with books. The way they are put together, the materials used, the purposes for which they are intended, are related to their time and

[2] See, e.g., Gen. 27:46–28:5; Exod. 5:22–6:1; 6:28–7:7; 7:25–8:7; 35:30–36:1; I Sam. 3:19–4:4; 6:19–7:2; Mark 8:34–9:1; I Cor. 10:1–11:1.

[3] See p. 67.

place. It is for this reason that study must always proceed with the historical situation clearly in mind.

A. Examining the Parts

We already have emphasized the fact that biblical books vary greatly in their structure—from lengthy, complex works (such as Luke-Acts) to simple creations (such as the book of Ruth or Paul's letter to Philemon). When we speak of "examining the parts" here, we mean examining the elements of which the whole is composed: major divisions, sections, and paragraphs. Actually sentences, clauses, phrases, and individual words belong to the "parts" too. These will be examined in their place, but the minimal unit on which the method to be described here can successfully be applied is the paragraph.

It should be said at the outset that the method of studying the parts which is now to be described should be used discriminatingly by the reader of the Bible. Not all parts of the Bible are worthy of paragraph-by-paragraph examination, to say nothing of sentence-by-sentence study. The richer and more closely packed the book, the more detailed the examination should be. Some books can be studied by sections, and some by major divisions. The initial survey should indicate how detailed the approach should be.

Three questions should be asked and answered in the study of any literary passage: (1) Exactly what does the passage say, and how does it say it? (2) What does it mean? (3) What is its significance for the reader and his contemporaries? Speaking affirmatively, we may say that accurate observation, thoughtful interpretation, unprejudiced evaluation, and practical application are required. Unfortunately our space will allow only a hurried look at these.

1. *Exactly what does the passage say, and how does it say it?*

When Luther put the Bible in the hands of his fellow countrymen with the invitation to read for themselves, he manifested a high degree of confidence in the common man. In view of the sectarianism which has run riot in the world since his time, much of which has stemmed from an inaccurate reading and interpretation of the Bible, it may not be impertinent to ask whether the average man is worthy of so much confidence. Educational psychologists have found that many adult Americans are practically nonreaders, even though they have had enough formal education to give them reasonable facility. Others plod along, getting the drift of what they read, but with little deep comprehension of the material offered. Much eludes the best of us, and not a little is distorted by our failure to observe exactly and to interpret properly.

Scientists will sit by the hour, or even by days, and watch the activity of insects, bacteria, or the stars. First impressions are always checked and rechecked before any conclusions are drawn. Great writers likewise observe the human scene accurately and continuously. George Herbert Palmer, a famous Harvard teacher, wrote:

> Once, after puzzling long over the charm of Homer, I applied to a learned friend and said to him, "Can you tell me why Homer is so interesting? Why can't you and I write as he wrote? Why is it that his art is lost, and that to-day it is impossible for us to awaken an interest at all comparable to his?"—"Well," said my friend, "I have often meditated on that, but it seems to come to about this: Homer looked long at a thing. Why," said he, "do you know that if you should hold up your thumb and look at it long enough, you would find it

immensely interesting?" Homer looks a great while at his thumb. He sees precisely the thing he is dealing with. He does not confuse it with anything else. It is sharp to him; and because it is sharp to him it stands out sharply for us over thousands of years.[4]

We must read the Bible with this kind of care. We then shall not affirm that it says what it does not say. Many sects, like the devil, quote scripture for their purposes, without taking the trouble to ask, What does the passage really say?

In the R.S.V. the revisers have helped us immeasurably in getting at the exact text of the original biblical books. As was explained in Chapter I, they have carefully weighed the variant readings from the many ancient manuscripts and rendered the resultant text in clear English. It would be better, of course, if every modern reader could work with the Scriptures in the languages in which they were originally written. Failing this, an accurate translation must serve. It is unforgivable to give loose attention to a text which is so important that countless men of past centuries have devoted their lives to copying and preserving it, and so relevant to our times that a committee of great scholars spent nearly two decades in searching out the meaning of every word.

What is it that one should observe in working with a part, be it a paragraph, a section, or a major division?

a) *What type of material is here before you?* See page 60 for a list of the various types. It is important for interpretation, as I have so often said, to keep in step with the character of one's subject matter.

[4] George Herbert Palmer and Alice Freeman Palmer, *The Teacher* (Boston and New York: Houghton Mifflin Company, 1908), p. 162. I owe this illustration to Dr. Vartan D. Melconian.

b) *Is the part composed of smaller units of material?* A major division will usually break down into sections. These sections may or may not be identical with the chapters as they have come down to us since the thirteenth century. Do not hesitate to take exception to the traditional chapter divisions. It is clear that they were created largely for convenience of reference and were not meant to be thought of as representing a systematic analysis of the text. Attention has already been called to the frequent overriding of chapter divisions in the R.S.V.[5]

Observation of the spacing in Paul's letter to the Romans leads one to regard 1:8–4:25 as a major division. Is this major unit composed of lesser units? A close attention to the thought content of the material will tell. In 1:8-17 we have a personal introduction, at the end of which is a statement of the theme of the letter (1:16-17). In 1:18 Paul plunges into a discussion of the sinfulness of the world and the retribution such sinfulness entails. This arraignment runs through 3:20 and consists of a treatment of the sins of the Gentiles (1:18-32) and the sins of the Jews (2:1–3:20). Beginning with 3:21, Paul sets forth the way of salvation (God's redeeming work in Jesus Christ) and validates this way of salvation by an appeal to the Old Testament. This brings us to 4:25, the end of the major division. We thus have the following analysis:

1:8-17 Personal introduction and statement of the theme
1:18–3:20 The world's need of salvation
  1:18-32 The sins of the Gentiles

[5] See p. 72, note 2.

2:1–3:20 The sins of the Jews
3:21–4:25 The way of salvation and its validity

Even paragraphs often have a structure of parts. I Pet. 4:12-19 deals with the Christian experience of suffering. The paragraph may be analyzed as follows:

4:12-13 Your attitude toward suffering—let it be rejoicing!
4:14-18 The ground of your suffering—let it be Christian!
4:19 Your conduct in suffering—let it be trustful well-doing!

Clues to the structure of a passage are often afforded by the connectives, as well as by the general movement of thought. Eph. 2 consists of two paragraphs, both of which divide into two parts. In chapter 2 the writer is discussing the change in the lives of the readers made by their acceptance of Jesus Christ as Saviour. In each paragraph the word "but" divides the material into contrasting parts. In 2:1-3 the readers' former sinful manner of life and God's judgment upon it is discussed, and in 2:4-10 their present favorable position before God as a result of his grace and their response of faith is set forth. Similarly, 2:11-22 describes, first, their former unfortunate position outside Christ and his community (2:11-12) and, second, their present full participation in the opportunities and benefits of the Christian community (2:13-22). Paragraphs can frequently be divided into their constituents by attention to these connectives: *and*, *but*, *because*, *for*, *since*, *so*, *therefore*, *hence*, *however*, *nevertheless*, *finally*. Ideas are always related to one another in some logical structure. The connectives tell you how they are related. In handling literature we must always think and study relatedly.

c) What are the important words around which the thought of the unit being studied revolves? The important words are those which cannot be sacrificed without a breakdown of meaning. They are like piers of a bridge; without them the whole structure would collapse. In many instances these words are repeated frequently. For example, one does not read far in the magnificent poetry of the Second Isaiah until he is aware that the meaning rides along on the back of great words: God, Creator, comfort, redeem, righteousness, salvation, servant, all flesh, covenant, idols, things to come. Make a list of the great words in the portion you are working on. Their precise meaning can wait, for the moment.

d) What features of the material are still puzzling to you? Make a list of them. It is helpful to distinguish clearly what you do understand from what you do not. You will probably not understand allusions to ancient customs and institutions, geographical and time notations, or ancient psychology and world views. By isolating these you can make a piece-by-piece attack on the passage, until the whole becomes clear.

2. *What does the passage mean?*

Up to this point you have been gathering significant facts about the unit under consideration. Now you are to look thoughtfully at these facts and with the help of your fellow explorers (in commentaries, lexicons, introductions to the Bible, etc.)[6] search out the author's meaning.

[6] See pp. 147-50.

The discovery of meaning results from the process of deep pondering over what we read, from putting questions to the material and to ourselves. Such questions will send us back to the material and to available books about the Bible for answers. The difference between observation of facts (what is said) and interpretation (what is meant) may be seen from an advertisement which appeared in the *New York Times* on April 10, 1940, in behalf of Mortimer J. Adler's *How to Read a Book.* Underneath a picture of an adolescent youth reading his first love letter appeared these words:

> This young man has just received his first love letter. He may have already read it three or four times, but he is just beginning. To read it as accurately as he would like, would require several dictionaries and a good deal of close work with a few experts on etymology and philology.
>
> However he will do all right without them.
>
> He will ponder over the exact shade of meaning of every word, every comma. She has headed the letter "Dear John." What, he asks himself, is the exact significance of those words? Did she refrain from saying "Dearest" because she was bashful? Would "My Dear" have sounded too formal?
>
> Jeepers, maybe she would have said "Dear So-and-So" to anybody!
>
> A worried frown will now appear on his face. But it disappears as soon as he really gets to thinking about the first sentence. She certainly wouldn't have written *that* to anybody!
>
> And so he works his way through the letter, one moment perched blissfully on a cloud, the next moment huddled miserably behind an eightball. It has started a hundred questions in his mind. He could quote it by heart. In fact, he will—to himself—for weeks to come.[7]

[7] Used by permission of the publishers, Simon and Schuster, Inc.

If people everywhere would read the Bible in this way—with complete absorption in the business of finding out what it really means—the shape of things to come would be appreciably altered.

What steps are involved in the process of discovering meaning?

a) *Immerse yourself in the passage by repeated readings,* until the words and ideas have taken possession of you, until they have become familiar friends rather than mere acquaintances. Bombard the passage with questions. This is not irreverent. It was written to tell you what you want to know about it.

b) *Search out the meaning of each of the crucial words you have listed.* Sometimes a concordance to the Bible is helpful. If you will look up all or many of the occurrences of a word in the Bible, some help may be gained toward determining the possible range of meanings it has. Preference must be given, as was pointed out in Chapter II, to meanings current in the author's time, and in every case the meaning required by the context must be decisive. A book such as *A Theological Word Book of the Bible*, edited by Alan Richardson, is worth its weight in gold to the serious student of the Bible. Help on the exact significance of important words will also be found in commentaries.

c) *Investigate the puzzling features listed.* You will need full information on ancient customs, institutions, world views and psychology. If your one-volume commentary is not sufficiently detailed, borrow from the local library one that more thoroughly treats the book being studied. You can hardly expect to understand the story of Abraham's intended offering of Isaac (Gen. 22) if you know nothing about the practice of child sacrifice among the Canaanites; or Paul's injunctions about the eating of meat offered to idols (I Cor. 8–10) if you are totally unfamiliar with the ancient situation.

d) *State in a sentence, or at most in a brief paragraph, the central idea of the paragraph, section, or major division on which you are working.* You have grasped the writer's meaning when you can put in your own words the heart of what he has said.

In the book of Daniel you will find from your initial survey of the whole that chapters 1–6 consist of a group of similar stories about Daniel and his friends in captivity in Babylonia. Chapters 7–12 are quite different in nature. They consist of visions containing prophecies about events yet to come. Let us suppose that you have concluded that chapters 1–6 break down into several sections, one of which is chapter 1. You might formulate the central idea of this chapter somewhat as follows: Because they were loyal to the food laws of God and their people, Daniel and his friends were rewarded by God with more health and successs than they would have enjoyed if they had taken the easy way and conformed to the practices of their heathen oppressors. This statement catches up most that is important in the chapter and prepares the way for the next step in the interpretative process.

e) *Investigate the author's purpose in the part.* This requires the relating of the part to the whole book and to the historical purposes that lay behind the creation of the book. You may not be able to do this accurately always, but you can make an attempt. At a later point in the reading procedure you will be in a position to refine your opinion.

Let us return to Dan. 1. Your survey of the whole book and your reading from a commentary or other secondary source about the historical situation out of which the book came will have led you to the following facts. The book was written about 165 B.C., during days of dreadful persecution in Palestine at the hands of a fanatical Syrian tyrant (Antiochus Epiphanes). This foul king tried to stamp out the Jewish religion. He forbade the Jews to circumcize their children, keep their ancestral food laws, and offer sacrifices in the temple to their God. He ordered them to destroy their Scriptures and to sacrifice pigs on altars dedicated to the worship of himself as the god Zeus. The writer of the book of Daniel wanted to exhort his fellow countrymen to resist the demands of this fanatic and to be loyal to their ancestral religion at all costs. The purpose of chapter 1 against this background can now be stated somewhat as follows: The writer wished to show his readers that defiance of Antiochus' commands and unswerving loyalty to God's laws concerning foods would pay off in the long run. This he accomplished by holding up the example of holy men of old, who were rewarded by God with more health and success than they would have enjoyed had they compromised their principles.

As other sections of the major division are taken up and their function in the total book defined, clarity of understanding will be greatly advanced.

3. *What is the significance of the passage for the modern reader and his contemporaries?*

We are not done with the Bible, nor is it done with us, when we have understood what it says and what it means. Though the books of the Bible were written for ancient people and deal with ancient problems, it has a message from God for *us*. This was stressed in Axiom VI.

How does this message from God come to us through the Bible? And will all readers receive the same message? Will this message help us both in our personal religious lives and with our social, political, and economic problems? If so, how? Profound questions, these! They are so profound that the Study Department of the World Council of Churches has sponsored conferences in the attempt to answer them and has published a book, written by participating scholars, embodying conclusions.[8] We can hardly hope to make a pin prick, to say nothing about scratching the surface, in the little space we have here. But let me venture a few suggestions.

a) *Keep your mind and heart open as you read and study, in order that you may inwardly apprehend the truth.* Christians of all ages have found that when they have come to the Bible thoughtfully and prayerfully, with a deep hunger in their hearts to feed on the Word of God, they have not gone away from the experience empty. In an hour of deep soul-searching over the sacred page, words seem to rise up and shout their message into the inmost recesses of one's being.

What does God say in such an experience? Does he tell one how to play the stock market so that one can double his money? Does he tell one the date of the coming of Christ and the end of the world? Christians as a whole have found that he speaks to them in the story of salvation which the Bible contains. They see that if God was in Christ reconciling the world unto himself, he was seeking to recon-

[8] Alan Richardson and Wolfgang Schweitzer (eds.), *Biblical Authority for Today* (Philadelphia: Westminster Press, 1951).

cile *them* unto himself, for they are part of that world. They see that they are standing in the presence of a holy God with unclean hands and impure hearts, and that they dwell in the midst of an unclean people. They find themselves driven to their knees in deep contrition and rising with cleansed consciences and renewed commitments. They feel impelled to join their Lord in preaching "good news to the poor," releasing "the captives," restoring "sight to the blind," and proclaiming "the acceptable year of the Lord" (Luke 4:18-19). God's word to us will be according to our need. It will be a very personal word, but often with large social consequences.

Will we find help from the Bible on our social, political, and economic problems? If by this we mean, Is there a detailed blueprint in the Bible in which God's will for human society in our time is expressed? the answer must be that there is not. There are in the Bible only many historical forms of social organization. The Sermon on the Mount is hardly what a confused and overly enthusiastic American writer at the beginning of the twentieth century claimed it to be: "the science of society . . . a treatise on political economy." About proper forms of social and political organization it has nothing to say. Whether capitalism or socialism is to be preferred cannot be *directly* determined from the Sermon on the Mount or the Bible as a whole.

What we may discover in the Bible is rather the moral and spiritual laws under which we live and to which we must be subject if we are to live well. That God is the Creator and Lord of life, to whose laws kings, governments, and the common man must be obedient; that God is equally interested in the welfare of every person on earth, so that it is an offense against him for persons to exploit other persons; that it is his will that we should have as much regard for the interests of our fellows as for our own and should assist them to fullness of life by every means available to us—all these and many more are considerations of great relevance for our social, political, and economic life. But they hardly constitute a pattern of organization. It is for us as free sons of the Father to devise patterns best suited to the conditions under which we live. A social system designed to meet the needs of ancient nomads, wandering from oasis to oasis, would hardly be adequate for the atomic age.

God will speak to us, if we will listen, about the matters of ultimate significance: where we came from and why we are here in this world; what laws govern our existence and what we should do when we have broken them; what goals we should set before ourselves; and what destiny lies before the race. It is his will that we should use the insights afforded us from the natural, social, and biological sciences, as well as from the Bible, in working out our practical problems. And it is worth remembering that we have been promised the illuminating, guiding presence of the Holy Spirit.

b) "*Test everything; hold fast what is good*" (I Thess. 5:21). Deep intuitions of truth must be subjected to certain tests. In I John 4:1 we read, "Test the spirits to see whether they are of God." The Bible gives no comfort to lazy minds!

Some devout people have come away from the Bible with curious notions. On the basis of Jer. 10:1-5 one religious group denounces the Christmas tree and forbids its use among its membership. Many sincere Americans and Britons believe that the Anglo-Saxon people are descendants of the ten lost tribes of Israel. How are we to escape the pitfalls into which so many have fallen?

In the first place we must check our intuitions evoked by reading the Bible with the body of truth as we know it from all sources. To put it in technical language, we may say that these intuitions must cohere in the structure of reality. God will never ask us to believe or do something which is out of line with that which he himself is, and out of harmony with the physical and moral laws of the universe. That which is true in science will agree with that which is true in the Bible. Our inner apprehensions must never be repugnant to sound reason.

Secondly we must check our insights against the conclusions of others who have experimented in the same areas. God and the truth have no favorites. We must beware of visions and revelations which would carry us out of the stream of historic Christian beliefs and experience. And we must remember that as Christians our touchstone is the life and teachings of Jesus.

Space forbids me to speak of other tests, but these are sufficient to make the point.

c) *Begin at once to obey the truth when it becomes clear to you that it really is truth.* There is only one thing to be done with truth, and that is to obey it. It cannot be filed away in the mind on a storage shelf until one feels like attending to it. We are not its master to handle it as we will; it is our master, and we are judged by it the moment it dawns upon us. "Walk while you have the light, lest the darkness overtakes you." (John 12:35.)

d) *Keep a list of unanswered questions for later consideration.* Many of the books of the Bible deal with the greatest questions ever to occupy the mind of man. It will take a lifetime of study to grasp the import of some of the magnificent passages that deal with them and to see even partially how the truth there set forth applies to us today. Do not be alarmed if you cannot fathom all mysteries at the beginning of your study. Remember that the scholars are peering along with you into the murky darkness out there in the hope of catching even a fleeting glimpse of the outskirts of God's ways!

B. Re-viewing the Whole Book

After you have worked through the book part by part—whether by paragraphs, by sections, or by major divisions—according to the procedure outlined above, you are ready for the third main step in the interpretation of a biblical book: an attempt to comprehend the whole as a totality of parts. The importance of this was stressed by Richard Green Moulton, a well-known literary scholar: "In the case of the higher literary forms the whole is a different thing from the sum of the parts. It is quite possible to have considered every detail of a literary work and yet to be far from understanding the work as a whole."[9] A human being is vastly more than an aggregate of feet, legs, torso, arms, and head. A scientist might study all of these one by one in great detail and be far from understanding man as a unitary being. He would miss, for example, the beliefs, fears, desires, and hopes by which a man lives.

Several steps are involved in re-viewing a book as a whole.

1. *Restate the central subject or message of the book and show how the major parts contribute to its presentation.* As an illustration let us look at Luke-Acts. It is clear that

[9] *The Bible at a Single View* (New York: The Macmillan Co., 1919), p. 103.

the Gospel according to Luke and the Acts of the Apostles constitute two volumes of one continuous work.[10] The central subject and the contribution of the parts to the development of this subject may be expressed as follows: [11]

THE SUBJECT OF LUKE-ACTS: The Gospel of God for the Whole World

Vol. I (Luke): As taught, lived, and accomplished (through his death and resurrection) by Jesus of Nazareth				Vol. II. (Acts): As spread throughout the Roman world by the witnessing of Jesus' followers		
CHAPTERS				CHAPTERS		
1–2 Preparation—Births of John the Baptist and Jesus	3:1–9:50 In Galilee	9:51–19:27 On the way to Jerusalem	19:28–24:53 In Jerusalem	1:1–8:3 In Jerusalem	8:4–12:25 In Judea and Samaria	13:1–28:31 To the end of the earth

A very long and complicated body of material has been summarized in this chart, in fact more than one fourth of the total text of the New Testament. A difficult body of material was purposely selected to indicate how one can see the skeleton that underlies the fleshy tissue, if he develops X-ray eyes.[12] In such a chart the eye can take in at a glance the major structural features of the material and understand how the whole is tied up logically. *One must be careful not to impose a scheme of organization on the book being studied.* The analysis must rise up from the

[10] See any standard introduction to the New Testament or A.B.C., p. 1094.

[11] From my booklet *A Leader's Guide to a Study of the Book of Acts* (Cincinnati: Woman's Division of Christian Service, The Methodist Church, 1951), p. 21, here slightly modified.

[12] A much simpler illustration is presented on p. 130.

material itself. It must describe accurately what the author actually did in his book, not what we wish he had done. Of course, we must not commit the other error of assuming from a superficial contact with the book that it consists of an agglomeration of words without discernible logic.

2. *Investigate the special themes that run like golden threads through the book.*

On page 66 it was suggested (as part of the initial survey) that one should be alert to an author's special interests. It was said that Luke tells us a good deal about the prayer life of Jesus and the early church, the Holy Spirit, and the social implications of the gospel. Jesus' attitudes toward money and its use, sex, and socio-religious and racial barriers are fully set forth. Each one is a rich vein of ore.

The writer of the Gospel according to John was especially interested in portraying the effect which Jesus had on various individuals and groups. Some believed and some disbelieved. By gathering together and thoughtfully studying all cases of belief and unbelief (from such standpoints as who believed or disbelieved, where such took place, how belief or unbelief is indicated, and the reason suggested for the attitude taken) one can gain many thrilling insights. It will be seen, for example, that there are various levels of belief in this Gospel. There was the kind possessed by the crowd in Jerusalem (2:23-25). These people saw the spectacular works done by Jesus and apparently acclaimed him Messiah, but only such a Messiah as was popularly expected. There was no deep understanding of his work or trust in his person. Then there were those who believed in the truth of what he said (8:30-31), a necessary stage on the way to complete discipleship. And, finally, there were some, like the man born blind, whose belief was so deep that they defended Jesus against his enemies and "worshiped him" (9:38). Full belief, according to this Gospel, involves the whole man: knowledge about Jesus' relationship to the Father (14:10; 17:7-8); obedience to his commands (14:15; 15:12-17); and intimate spiritual-moral fellowship (9:38; 15:1-11; 17:20-23).

In First John the writer suggests a number of tests by which one can know whether or not he is a Christian: the test of love (2:9-11; 3:10, 14; 4:7, 16); the test of conduct (1:6; 3:4-10); and the test of belief (4:2, 15; 5:1, 5, 10, 12). In studying the second test one will encounter the important problem concerning the relationship of the Christian to sin, and by the help of the commentaries one will discover that the kind of sinning referred to in 3:6 relates to a prevailing habit, not primarily to an individual act.

It is impossible here to do more than suggest the possibilities in the study of special themes. You will discover the golden threads for yourself, if your eyes are sharp. The process of investigating them may be briefly described as follows:

a) Locate every passage in the book dealing with one theme. A concordance can be of help here. Look up the word principally involved.

b) Group the passages together according to what they contain. If you are studying the prayer life of Jesus, some passages will tell you about where he prayed, some about when he prayed, others about what he prayed for, and still others about the results of his prayers. The questions to ask of the material are Who, When, Where, What, How, and Why?

c) Consult your commentaries for help on difficult passages.

d) Draw up thoughtful conclusions *in written form.* You will fail to be specific otherwise.

e) Check these conclusions against the results achieved by scholars, if you can. Most commentaries have introductions in which the special themes are discussed.

f) Consider carefully the value of these conclusions for yourself and for others.

3. *Relate the message of the entire book to the historical situation which gave rise to it.*

This will involve asking yourself, What meaning did the book as a whole have for its first readers? How did it speak to their needs?

Consider again Luke-Acts. During the initial survey we would have learned some things about Theophilus and other intended readers, the conditions in the church and in the world at the time when this two-volume work was written, the identity of the author, and the like. We would have found that about A.D. 90 Christians were being accused by their enemies of being revolutionists and thus enemies of the state, for they were proclaiming the return of King Jesus, who would destroy the Roman Empire and all human authority. Someone needed to show that Christianity was not a subversive political movement. It was not politics at all. It was, rather, good news from God concerning the salvation of all men—Romans as well as Jews—a gospel which had been received joyfully by an ever-growing company of people from every nation under heaven. Furthermore, it needed to be pointed out that when the early preachers of this gospel were tried by governors and kings, they could find no fault in them. Christianity is God's act in the world, not man's. Luke-Acts is thus in part a defense of Christianity before its accusers.

But if the gospel is for all men, then all men should hear and accept it. The author obviously wished to convert those who were suspicious of the church. He has marshaled a great body of evidence to show that God was at work in this movement from its very beginning, and even before. He probably hoped that his work would be read by many open-minded Gentiles, who would hear the message and believe.

The work had yet another purpose. In its preface (Luke 1:1-4) it is stated that many accounts of Jesus' words and deeds were in circulation. It is implied that the author believed he could improve on them by giving a more "orderly account." He probably wanted to edify the church by presenting it a better description of its historical foundations. We now see that the work had three purposes: apologetic, evangelistic, and historical. It filled a practical need in the life of the church of its day.

4. *Study any remaining obscurities in the book in the light of your knowledge of the whole.*

While not all difficulties will vanish when approached in the light of the total book, many of them will. Says Moulton, "If there are obscurities, we must sweep through the book a second and a third time—or, it may be, a twentieth and thirtieth time—and watch the obscurities vanish in the light of the book as a whole."[13]

5. *Summarize the contribution which the study of this biblical book has made to you.*

How can you use the helpful material in it for the benefit of others?

In conclusion it ought to be emphasized again that the method of reading set forth in this and the preceding chapter

[13] *Op. cit.*, p. 103.

cannot be used with equal success on all biblical books. It is not intended for books which are not substantially unified. These require a different approach, to be described in the next chapter. But even in those books which are fundamentally one, the reader will need to be discriminating in his use of the method. Not all points will be worth investigating in a given book. If you find you are not in pay dirt, gather up your tools and move on to another spot and dig there! Before long you will know how to size up a biblical book on the first reading and be able to decide quickly how much of the reading method to follow through.

CHAPTER FIVE

Reading the Nonunified Books

IT WAS POINTED OUT IN CHAPTERS I AND II THAT THE BOOKS OF THE BIBLE ARE OF MANY LITERARY TYPES AND present many points of view. Among them are such widely different materials as the love ballads of the Song of Solomon and the sublimely religious poetry of Isa. 40–66, and such different attitudes as the exclusiveness of Nahum and Esther and the inclusiveness of Ruth and Jonah.

However, as we read them all thoughtfully, it becomes clear that in a real sense they belong together and form a true and living whole. We can understand how the unity and the variety go together when we realize that these are books of a people, that they grew out of its life. That life passed through many stages and had many forms and interests, just as ours today. We in America have books of widely varying outlook and form, but all reflect in one way or another American culture and are held together by it. The binding element was much stronger in Hebrew culture, of course, for life was largely dominated by the cohesive power of a great religious faith.

There is a fascinating story behind the formation of our Bible. It reaches back to the childhood of the Hebrews. Their literature at first was a folk literature. Folk literature results from a sort of spontaneous generation. Moments of high emotion are caught up in lyric poetry by unnamed shepherds. Tribal lore is passed down in rhythmic cadence from father to son. Fables, riddles, and pithy sayings constitute the course of study in the school of life. Some of the writings of the Old Testament contain much of this kind of material; and the more of it present, the less unified the book that enshrines it.

In later and more sophisticated periods Israel produced literary men, who set about deliberately to create books. By the time of the writer of Ecclesiastes (about 200 B.C.) so many books were in existence that this tired philosopher felt impelled to say, "Of making many books there is no end, and much study is a weariness of the flesh" (12:12). Folk literature is apt to be crude in words and unpolished in form, but it is packed with emotion and therefore highly moving. It knows none of the artificialities that mark the deliberate creations of the "experts." However, the "experts" put thoughts together more logically, if not always more effectively. Since their writings are structurally superior, they are on the whole more easily read by modern Westerners than the more spontaneous creations of earlier periods.

Chapters III and IV have been devoted to a description of the method of reading those books of the Bible which are fundamentally or substantially unified. It will be noted from the list on page 55 that these are prose writings. Though there are folk materials imbedded in some of the Old Testament books there listed (notably in Genesis,

Exodus, Numbers, Judges, and First and Second Samuel), all are at least substantially unified. Scholars are agreed that *in their present form* all these books were put together since the beginning of the exile in Babylonia (587 B.C.) and thus belong to the period of deliberate literary activity, not to the more spontaneous earlier period. The books of the New Testament are products of Gentile Christianity. They were written in a literary age. Though some of them enshrine traditional materials (such as the words and deeds of Jesus in the Gospels), almost all are quite well unified.

It will be seen from the list of nonunified books that virtually all are poetic or predominantly poetic. This is not to say that all of them therefore consist of early folk materials, for poetry was written throughout the Old Testament period. Psalms and Proverbs appear to contain some of these early materials, and several of the books of the earlier prophets (Amos, Hosea, Micah, and Jeremiah) contain oracles (proclamations of the will of God) which possess all the vigor and rugged splendor of folk literature. The writings of the later prophets (Ezekiel, the Second Isaiah, Malachi, Joel, and others) show a conscious striving for literary effect.

The nonunified books of the Old Testament fall into three main classes: the prophetic books (Isaiah, Jeremiah, Ezekiel, Hosea, Joel, Amos, Obadiah, Micah, Nahum, Habakkuk, Zephaniah, Haggai, Zechariah, and Malachi); the poetical books proper (Psalms, Lamentations, and Song of Solomon); and the wisdom books (Job, Proverbs, and Ecclesiastes). The book of James is the New Testament counterpart of Proverbs. Second Corinthians is widely believed to contain parts of three letters written by Paul, which somehow became joined together at the time when the letters were first collected, or shortly thereafter.[1] All these books are made up of pieces of varying lengths. Some are arranged more logically than others, but none is fully unified.

How shall we treat books of this sort? To what extent, if at all, is the procedure set forth in Chapters III and IV applicable? Before attempting to answer these questions, it will be well to set forth a general covering principle. It has been formulated and illustrated profusely by Julian Price Love in his book *How to Read the Bible*. He says, "The best of all ways to read the Bible with satisfaction is by *units of thought*." [2] He defines a unit of thought as "any passage, however long or short, that naturally belongs together, and should be read and understood together because it deals with just one theme." [3] If we cannot deal with the total book as a unit, we can come to grips with the many units of which it is composed.

Unfortunately, I cannot present here detailed suggestions for reading all the nonunified books. I shall have to illustrate the general method and let you apply it to the other books listed in this class. For this purpose I shall use the prophetic books and the Psalms.

A. Reading the Prophetic Books

Many Christians of our day have very little appreciation of the Old Testament. In fact, so little do they know it and value it, that they would be quite happy to see it dropped from the canon. Long ago a heretic by the name of Marcion (second century A.D.) advocated this, but fortunately the

[1] See A.B.C., pp. 1169, 1202-3.

[2] P. 14. Italics Love's.

[3] *Ibid.*

counsels of better minds prevailed, and the Old Testament was retained.

To anyone who feels as Marcion did, many things can be said. One of the chief of these is that the Old Testament was the Bible of Jesus. From his many allusions to it we know that his mind was saturated with its language and ideas. He won victory over temptation by quoting apt verses to his adversary, and he found in its pages a definition of his role in God's plan for the world. We may say without fear of overstating the evidence that these books constituted one of the most formative influences in his personal spiritual growth. The earliest Christians likewise searched out the secrets of the Old Testament and drew from it inspiration and courage for their difficult missionary endeavors. The Old Testament was handed down in the church because it was continuously found to be of inestimable religious value.

It is agreed on all sides that the high point of Old Testament religion is to be seen in the prophetic books. It was in Isaiah and Jeremiah that deep called unto deep in the soul of Jesus. In Isa. 61:1-2 he found his mission exactly defined (Luke 4:16-21) and in 52:13–53:12 a soul-girding explanation of the significance of his approaching death. By joining with these Jer. 31:31-34 he viewed with a degree of equanimity the failure of his national "back-to-God" crusade and cast the issue in faith into the hands of the God who brings victory out of apparent defeat. If the prophets could speak so mightily to Jesus, we can scarcely afford to ignore them.

In determining how these books should be read it is necessary to understand how they came to be what they are. The early prophets of Israel, such as Samuel, Nathan, Elijah, and Elisha, wrote nothing, as far as we know. Their utterances were formulated for specific situations and were cast in poetic form, in a kind of ecstatic chanting. That the emotional content in the experience and words of these prophets was high is clearly evident from such passages as I Sam. 10:1-13. They associated in bands, sometimes as many as four hundred in one group (I Kings 22:6). In certain periods many of them were charlatans, who, for a consideration, told inquirers what they wanted to hear (Jer. 23:16-32). Others were blinded by extreme patriotism. They always predicted success for Israel on the ground of its election by God as his special people. But out of this general movement, in spite of its shortcomings, emerged a succession of great spirits who saw deep into the mind of God and proclaimed his word exactly as they received it. These men did not say, "It shall be well with you" (Jer. 23:17), but they "prophesied war, famine, and pestilence" (Jer. 28:8) and "proclaimed my words to my people, and . . . turned them from their evil way" (Jer. 23:22).

Amos (about 750 B.C.) apparently was the first prophet to put his utterances into writing. Not all of the book that bears his name can be attributed to him, however. This book, as do many of the prophetic books, contains four types of material: oracles or proclamations, much as they were originally delivered (chapters 1–6); autobiographical pieces (7:1-9; 8:1–9:8); biographical material (7:10-17); and oracles later in date than the prophet's time (9:9-15, and other pieces here and there in the book). For exactly how much of this written material Amos is directly responsible cannot be said, though hardly for more than the first two types. Men who revered his memory and wanted to perpetuate his unforgettable words put his book together in its present form, adding material of their own.

The writing of the book of Jeremiah came about in much the same way. We know that Jeremiah dictated to his secretary, Baruch, two scrolls of his prophecies. The first was burned in disdain by King Jehoiakim (see Jer. 36). The second apparently forms the basis of chapters 1–25 of our present book. To this Baruch added much biographical material (in chapters 26–52). Later editors added passages here and there.[4] The commanding figure of Jeremiah stands behind the whole book, but only parts of it come directly from him.

Since the prophetic books were put together more or less gradually, often over a period of considerable time, we would expect to find in them a somewhat loose arrangement of materials. Among the best arranged are Amos, Ezekiel, Haggai, and Joel. More unsystematic are Hosea, Isaiah, and Jeremiah. Fortunately, some of them (notably Jeremiah, Ezekiel, and Haggai) present frequent time and place notations, from which one can start in reordering the materials for reading. When such notations are not present, it is difficult indeed to put the pieces in their proper historical order.

It should be obvious by now that the main fact to be borne in mind in reading the prophetic books is that they are loosely, rather than closely knit together. They cannot be treated as wholes in the way we treated the unified or substantially unified books. How then, in specific terms, shall we read them?

1. *Begin with a study of the times in which the prophet lived.* Since the prophets never spoke in vague generalities but always had the word of the Lord in moments of per-

[4] For details see one of the Introductions to the Old Testament listed on p. 149.

sonal and national crisis, their utterances obviously cannot be understood until we know something about the situations in which they lived and spoke. It would be difficult indeed to make much of the collected papers of Franklin Delano Roosevelt without a knowledge of his times: the great depression, the rise of totalitarianisms around the world, and the Second World War.

How can we get an understanding of a prophet's period? There are two sources of information—biblical and nonbiblical. Important data will be available in the prophetic book itself. Other biblical books, such as Second Kings, Second Chronicles, Ezra, Nehemiah, and the writings of other prophets of the same period, may help. Nonbiblical sources include archaeological materials from inside and outside Israel, and Egyptian, Babylonian, and Greek writings. It is difficult, if not impossible, for the beginner to dig out by himself the important matter in these many sources; hence, he will need to make much use of secondary sources.

However, if the prophetic book to be read is relatively short, it should be read through *at the outset* for whatever information it may yield about the period. Two types of data should be looked for: historical references that will help to place the prophet and his utterances chronologically, and descriptions—direct or indirect—of conditions during his life and ministry. From the sins denounced will come insight into the nature of his situation.

When evidence from the book itself has been exhausted, turn to A.B.C. (the "Introduction" to the particular book being read) for supplementary information. Look up the references in other biblical books cited. To help you sharpen up the historical situation in your mind, write a summarizing paragraph on the subject in your notebook.

If the prophetic book is long and involved (like Isaiah, Jeremiah, and Ezekiel), it will be best to start with A.B.C. directly. But maintain as much contact as possible with your biblical sources by looking up all references given in A.B.C. As above, write a summarizing paragraph on the prophet's times.

You should avoid reading at this point those sections of the "Introduction" that discuss the prophet's teaching, theology, or contribution. You are going to examine these for yourself, and you do not want or need predigested food. Anyhow, without more direct contact with the prophetic book the comments will mean little to you. After you have completed the reading process on the book, you can return to these portions for comparison with your own results.

2. *Investigate the arrangement of materials in the book.* If the book is short or relatively short, read it through for indications of systematic grouping of the oracles. Then turn to the "Introduction" in A.B.C. for comparison and supplementation. If one of the longer prophets is to be read, go directly to A.B.C. for help.

It would not be hard to discover that the book of Joel falls into two divisions: the first (1:2–2:27) consisting of a description of a terrible locust plague and its consequences; and the other (2:28–3:21) a prediction concerning the future. Even the generally disorganized book of Hosea may be divided into two parts: the personal experiences of the prophet, intermingled with reflections on the condition of Israel (chapters 1–3); and Israel's sins, coming punishment, and promise of restoration to God's favor (chapters 4–14). Remember that in the nonunified books structure is only editorial arrangement. This structure may not help us much in understanding the prophet's life and work. The real job is yet to be done—getting the historical occasion and the proper proclamations of the prophet together. But it is worth while to know how the early editor of the book arranged his material.

3. *Relate the various portions of the book to their proper historical background.* Unfortunately, even the biblical experts cannot do this entirely satisfactorily, for sufficient evidence is many times lacking. But we should keep the goal in mind, even though we shall never reach it.

The importance of this is clearly obvious in such a book as Jeremiah. This prophet's ministry extended over the reigns of five Judean kings, a period of about forty years. His prophecies are not chronologically arranged in the book; hence, we must assign them as nearly as possible to the reigns of the respective kings, so that we can see them against the conditions that called them forth. This sort of rearrangement the beginner cannot do for himself. He must seek help in A.B.C., introductions to the Old Testament, and the detailed individual commentaries.

4. *Project yourself as far as possible into each situation in which the prophet spoke.* Imagine the circumstances—the place, the person or persons addressed, the bystanders, the speaker (his dress, manner, temper, etc.). Determine exactly what was said and why. Do not be afraid to use your imagination. These books will come alive if you do!

5. *Pay special attention to the central notes in the oracles of the prophets.* What is it that they emphasize most? What is their view of God, of man and his deeds, of the proper God-man and man-man relationship? What have they to say about the future? Keep a page in your notebook for each of these subjects and gather data as you read. When you have finished, summarize what you have found and compare

it with the discussion on these points in the "introduction" to each book in A.B.C.

6. *Attempt to evaluate the contribution of each prophet you study to the life and destiny of his nation.* What would Israel have been like had he not been born? To what extent did he influence other prophets? In what way, if any, did he prepare the way for the coming of Jesus and the rise of Christianity? [5] These are weighty questions. You will not be able to answer them fully, but it will do you good to think about them. Compare your conclusions with the comments in A.B.C. and elsewhere.

7. *What of importance for our day is present in the words and deeds of these ancient prophets?* Be specific. Would their politics, economics, and social views really work today? Or is their chief significance to be found in their view of God and his general spiritual-moral requirements? Or are God's requirements always specific and individual? What are we to think of their promises of a glorious national future in Palestine? To what extent was their prediction of future events "inspired"? Ask questions and keep on asking questions. These will send you out on searches for answers.

B. Reading the Book of Psalms

Jesus and early Christians appear to have loved the Psalms as much as the prophetic writings. He and his disciples lifted their voices in the Hallel (Ps. 113–118) at the Last Supper (Matt. 26:30). While he hung on the cross, he meditated on the Twenty-second Psalm (Mark 15:34), and his final earthly words constituted a breathed quotation

[5] Attention to the cross references at the bottom of pages of the R.S.V. will lead you to judgments concerning the extent of his influence.

of Ps. 31:5: "Into thy hands I commit my spirit" (Luke 23:46). The hymns sung by Paul and Silas in prison were doubtless psalms (Acts 16:25). Paul urged the Christians at Colossae to "sing psalms and hymns and spiritual songs with thankfulness in your hearts to God" (Col. 3:16). By the time of Jerome (about A.D. 400) Christians everywhere were singing psalms. This venerable translator of the Bible into Latin, in a letter from Bethlehem, wrote:

> Wherever you turn, the labourer at the plough sings Alleluia: the toiling reaper beguiles his work with Psalms: the vine-dresser as he prunes the vine with his curved pruning-hook sings something of David's. These are the songs of this province: these, to use the common phrase, are its love ditties: these the shepherd whistles; these are the labourer's implements.[6]

Candidates for ordination and for ecclesiastical preferment in the early Middle Ages were required to know the whole Psalter by heart, and various persons made a practice of repeating all of it every day. Martin Luther called the Psalter "a Bible in miniature" and said that in it "all things which are set forth more at length in the rest of the Scriptures are collected into a beautiful manual of wonderful and attractive brevity." [7]

Many of us since childhood have walked beside the still waters with the Shepherd of the Twenty-third Psalm and have found the God of Jacob our refuge when the mountains were shaking in the heart of the sea (Ps. 46). But probably not many of us could recite more than a few of

[6] Cited in A. F. Kirkpatrick, *The Book of Psalms* (Cambridge: University Press, 1902), p. *c*.

[7] *Ibid.*, p. *cvi*.

the psalms by heart. We are poorer than we know because of our neglect of this "Bible in miniature."

In the form in which the psalms lie before us in the Psalter they comprise five books, probably in imitation of the Pentateuch.[8] A study of the contents of these "books" soon convinces one that the division is artificial, for the psalms in these groupings do not cohere logically. There is no reason, for example, for separating psalms 106 and 107. Both recount God's wonderful acts in history and obviously belong together. The appearance of the same psalm twice in the Psalter with only slight variations (14=53; 40:13-17=70; 57:7-11+60:5-12=108); such notations as that in 72:20 where it is said that "the prayers of David, the son of Jesse, are ended," though other psalms are attributed to David in later sections; the variation in the divine name in Books I and II; and the assignment of psalms to the "Sons of Korah" (Ps. 42–49) and to "Asaph" (50, 73–83)—all lead inescapably to the conclusion that the Psalter is a great collection of smaller collections. It is not organized according to subjects as is a modern hymnbook but is somewhat like the result one would get from joining Baptist, Methodist, and Presbyterian hymnbooks end to end without bothering to eliminate duplicate songs and to rearrange the whole. It is therefore confusing to try to read the Psalter in the order in which the individual psalms now lie.

The Psalter is by no means the easiest part of the Bible to read and understand. The ecstatic language of oriental poetry, the many cryptic allusions to ideas, attitudes, customs, and places, the curious parallelism of members characteristic of Hebrew poetry, the lack of information about the authors and their time and place of writing, and

[8] Book I, 1–41; II, 42–72; III, 73–89; IV, 90–106; V, 107–150.

many other difficulties hinder understanding by the Western reader. But the rewards from perusing the Psalms are so great that the courageous soul will not be turned back. What helps for reading them may be suggested?

1. *Read a general introduction to the Psalms for necessary background material.* The "Introduction" in A.B.C., pages 509-515, will constitute a solid beginning. Hebrew terms and technical matters in this "Introduction" may be passed by and attention fixed on the present organization of the Psalter, the steps in its formation, the problems of authorship and date, the poetic structure, and the classification of the psalms. The comments on the idea of God, the varieties of religious experience in the Psalter, and the religious values for today should be held over for later consideration. What is wanted is basic information of a kind that will assist one in *beginning* the reading. Conclusions will come later.

2. *Read the psalms in a sequence that takes account of their basic types.* Commentators have attempted to classify the psalms from many different points of view. One might group them according to their subject matter, according to the moods of the soul they express, or according to the situations today in which the various psalms would be appropriate. Contemporary scholars, following the lead of a German authority, Hermann Gunkel, tend to classify them according to their use at the time of their origin. Gunkel holds that psalms originally were created to accompany various acts of worship: individual acts (such as the presentation of offerings at the sanctuary) and group acts (such as community fasting on special fast days). The types of psalms are therefore as numerous as the types of occasions on which individuals and the community worshiped.

With the passing of time the types became mixed through changes in the character of the temple ritual, the influence of gifted individuals (prophets and wise men) who expressed their new insights in the old forms, and the advancing sense of the dramatic in Israel's literature and religion. Intricate antiphonal liturgies were created, in which many types were included. Undoubtedly the psalms were sung in the homes and about the daily labors, though their place was pre-eminently in individual and corporate worship in the temple. Through such informal singing the springs of the soul were continuously fed.

Though not all scholars today are in agreement with Gunkel's conclusions concerning the origin of the psalms and their basic types, most experts in this area follow his lead. His basic scheme is here adopted, with modifications and refinements suggested by Elmer A. Leslie.[9]

Type 1: Hymns

Hymns are songs of praise sung by individuals or groups at a sacred festival in the presence of the assembled congregation. Their purpose is to give thanks to God for his many benefits, to extol his character and his deeds. Hymns, as Gunkel says, "are sung for God alone." [10] The hymn "represents the deepest and noblest religious need of man, to kneel in the dust and worship that which is higher than himself." [11]

There are many kinds of hymns. Leslie enumerates and expounds them under the following captions:

[9] *The Psalms* (New York and Nashville: Abingdon-Cokesbury Press, 1949).

[10] *What Remains of the Old Testament* (New York: The Macmillan Company, 1928), p. 75.

[11] *Ibid.*, p. 74.

General Hymns of Praise (117, 150)
Hymns of Zion (48, 87, 46, 76)
Hymns of Pilgrimage (84, 122)
Hymns of Great Individuals (103, 111, 145)
Hymns, Songs, and Prayers for the Hebrew New Year (134, 47, 68, 93, 96, 97, 98, 99, 33, 149, 2, 21, 72, 101, 110, 132, 65, 67, 118, 124, 53, 82, 85, 123, 125, 126, 129)
Hymns of the Revelation of God
  In Nature (8, 19:1-6, 29, 104, 147, 148)
  In History (78, 105, 106, 114)
  In the Law (19:7-14, 119)

In reading the hymns you should forget yourself entirely and let your spirit be carried on the wings of song into the very presence of God, and there bow in adoration.

Type 2: Liturgies

In this type the hymn is put to special liturgical use. Liturgies are fairly complicated affairs: there is speaking and singing back and forth, from person to person and group to group. The pattern is frequently question, answer, and concluding blessing. Leslie lists four kinds of liturgies:

Liturgies of Entrance (15, 24, 100)
Liturgies of Praise and Thanksgiving (113, 115, 135, 136)
Prophetic Liturgies (50, 75, 81, 95)
Liturgy of Supplication (121)

Liturgies call for the use of imagination on the part of the modern reader. He must visualize the occasions and hear the antiphonal chanting. In reading Ps. 15, for example, one must imagine a company of pilgrims standing at the entrance to the temple and inquiring concerning the terms of admission into that holy place:

> O Lord, who shall sojourn in thy tent?
> Who shall dwell on thy holy hill?

From within the gates comes the answer of the priests:

> He who walks blamelessly, and does what is right,
> and speaks truth from his heart. . . .

After the pilgrims have moved inside, the officiating priest pronounces over them the Lord's blessing in words of assurance:

> He who does these things shall never be moved.

In the liturgies both form and content are worthy of special attention. In the Prophetic Liturgies the characteristic notes of Israel's great ethical prophets appear, indicating the extent to which the prophetic conception of God and the world enriched the worship experiences of the people.

Type 3: Laments of the People of Israel

Israel was dogged by misfortune most of her days. Famine, pestilence, invasion, national devastation and exile, calamities of nature—all were occasions of national lamentation. Assembling in the temple, clad in sackcloth and ashes, people and priests would pour out their complaint before God. They would remind him of his obligations to his covenant people and earnestly implore his help. On these occasions no food or drink could be taken, marital relationships were forbidden, and ordinary business was suspended. The worshipers would rend their garments, sprinkle dust and ashes on their bodies, fall upon the ground, and cry out in anguish to God. The priests would blow trumpets, cover the altar with sackcloth, and weep loudly as they stood before the altar. The choirs intoned lamentations.

As a whole the national laments are not particularly stimulating reading to the average present-day Christian. There are beautiful passages in them, however, if one is willing to search them out. The members of this type are Ps. 9, 10, 12, 36, 44, 58, 60, 74, 77, 79, 80, 83, 90, 94:1-15, 108, and 137. Ps. 90 alone would repay all the effort expended in exploring this group.

Type 4: Psalms About the King

Psalms were sung on days when events in the life of the Hebrew king were celebrated: his accession to the throne, his birthday, his marriage, his dedication of the sanctuary, his recovery from illness, his victory over his enemies, his death. In them health, prosperity, victory, and justice were besought. The psalms belonging to this type are 18, 20, 45, 61, 63, 89, and 144:1-11.

Type 5: Songs of Individual Thanksgiving

What the testimony meeting was to early Methodism, the thank-offering occasion in the temple was to Israel. When a Hebrew had been delivered from some mortal trouble, he would bring his relatives and friends to the temple, present his offering, and sing his song of gratitude in their presence. The song usually contained an introduction in which the purpose of the singer was declared, followed by an account of the trouble which he had experienced, an acknowledgment of the deliverance by God, and some reference to the thank-offering being presented. Psalms belonging to this group are 23, 30, 32, 34, 40:1-11,

66, 92, 107, 116, 138, 139, and 146. The reader will not easily exhaust the riches of these songs.

Type 6: Prayers of the Falsely Accused, Sick, and Penitent

Leslie divides this type into two ("Prayers of the Falsely Accused" and "Prayers of the Sick and the Penitent"), but in the interest of brevity we may well combine them. They are all "laments of individuals," to use Gunkel's term. In these psalms (indicated by Leslie as 3, 4, 5, 6, 7, 11, 13, 17, 22, 23, 25, 26, 27, 28, 31, 35, 38, 39, 41, 42, 43, 51, 52, 54, 55, 56, 57, 59, 62, 64, 69, 70, 71, 86, 88, 94:16-23, 102, 109, 120, 130, 140, 141, 142, and 143) it is evident that the psalmist regards himself as standing close to death because of sickness or the plots of his enemies. Occasionally he seems to be on trial or in prison. In the time of trouble he comes to the sanctuary with a sacrifice and there pours out his heart to God. The modern reader will find his own soul distresses mirrored in these psalms, though he will draw back from the vitriolic attitude expressed toward personal enemies. The prayers for cleansing from personal sin, such as Ps. 51, have profoundly influenced prayers of repentance through the centuries.

Type 7: Songs of Trust and of Wisdom

The songs of trust are 16, 91, and 131. Gunkel lists these as a subclass of laments of the individual. But Leslie sees in them "a trilogy of trust such as give rich, and at the same time varied, expression to this most important aspect of religious experience,"[12] and therefore deserving of sep-

[12] *Op. cit.*, p. 404.

arate classification. The "songs tinged with the temper of Hebrew wisdom" are 37, 49, 73, 112, 127, 128, 133, 144:12-15, and 1. These psalms deal with the problem which was of vital concern to the wise men of Israel: God's government of the world—whether he undergirds those who serve him and are righteous. There were many times when it seemed that the wicked were better off than the righteous. How could this be explained on the supposition that God was both good and all-powerful? Among these psalms are some of the finest in the Psalter.

It is not likely that you will want to read all the psalms, unless you wish to make this a special project. In Chapter VII good representatives of the various types are listed. By reading them type by type and bearing in mind the class characteristics of each, your appreciation of the Psalter will be greatly increased.

3. *Pay attention to the structure of a psalm.* Clues to meaning are frequently to be found in the *form* of an artistic creation. Poems are not simply words strung together; they are ideas built together in logical relationships.

Gunkel points out that the hymn in its purest form contains first an introduction in which the singer enjoins praise of the Lord. He may call on his own soul, his hearers, the nation as a whole, the earthly creation, and even beings other than man to praise the Lord.[13] The introduction is followed by the main part of the hymn, in which the reasons for praising God are given.[14] At the end a formal conclusion is frequently to be found. This usually bears

[13] See 103:1; 95:1-2; 117:1.

[14] 103:2-19; 95:3-5; 117:2*ab*.

much the same form as the introduction.[15] By no means all the hymns as they now lie in the Psalter exhibit these parts, for they entered into combination with other types in the course of time. But these fundamental elements should be noted when they occur.

The liturgies likewise present marked structural features. In fact, they cannot be understood at all if one is not alert to their form. In some of them the pattern runs: question, answer, blessing. Examine Ps. 15 and see these elements in verses 1, 2-5*b*, and 5*c*.

The songs of individual thanksgiving usually divide into introduction, narration (of previous condition, the calling on the Lord, the deliverance), acknowledgment (of God's deliverance), and announcement (concerning the thank-offering the psalmist is bringing). See, for example, Ps. 116, where the units as given above are verses 1-2, 3-7, 8-11, and 12-19.

You must not expect rigid conformity to pattern in all members of a type. The psalms are too fluid for that. Types become mixed. Praise has an unrestrained quality; it will not be rigidly shackled in forms and patterns. But attention to the general movement of a psalm is indispensable to real understanding.

4. *State the central idea of the psalm in a brief phrase.* Professor Leslie has done this admirably for every psalm of the Psalter. Consider some of them:

Psalm 1 Life's Two Ways
8 The Symphony of the Heavens
32 The Glad Consciousness of God's Forgiveness

[15] 103:20-22; 95:6-7; 117:2*c*. Psalm 95 is a prophetic liturgy whose first element (1-7*c*) is a hymn of pure type. The remainder of the psalm contains the prophetic teaching (7*d*-11).

73 The Place of Worship in the Solution of Life's
Problems

This will require you to penetrate to the very heart of the psalm, and it will give you something to remember the psalm by.

5. *Record the principal teachings of each psalm.* The real meat is, after all, the thought content. What does the psalm tell us about God, man, sin, salvation, and our obligations toward God and man? Here also, as in studying the prophets, you should enter your discoveries in your notebook, so that you can summarize them when you have finished.

6. *Above all else, consider the significance of the psalms for your personal life and the life of our times.* The book of Psalms is a book of worship. If your reading of the psalms does not lead you to raise your voice with every created thing in praise of God, the Creator and Redeemer, you have yet to come into the kind of personal knowledge of the psalmists' God that gave rise to these masterpieces of the inner life. And you will want to know what God requires of his servants. In evaluating and making your applications bear in mind what was said on pages 82-87.

It should be apparent by now that the chief factors in determining how biblical books should be read are the character and relationship of the units contained. When a whole book is a unit, our problem is to see it first as a whole, then as a structure of parts, and finally once more as a totality. When dealing with disorganzied or loosely organized material, our approach cannot be to the whole book but must be to the individual units. These we try to arrange in some sort of pattern, be it historical-chronological (as in the prophetic writings) or logical (as in the psalms). Much of what was said in Chapter IV about the procedure involved in examining the parts will apply to the reading of individual units of nonunified literature. The interrelationships of the units, as they now lie in the various books, will not, of course, be so significant.

It will take more patience to read the nonunified than the unified or substantially unified books. But the effort will be richly repaid. The thundering voice of Amos and the plaintive, appealing tones of Hosea and Jeremiah are caught up in the mighty crescendos of the psalmists until the whole universe is set quivering. Though the wise men of Israel sing with somewhat scratchier voices and sometimes even off key (as in Ecclesiastes), they help carry along the song of redemption until the angelic choir takes it up over the shepherds' field at Bethlehem. You will not want to miss a single aria or chorus of this great oratorio!

CHAPTER SIX

Applying the Methods of Reading

ANYONE WHO PREPARES FOR TAKING UP A SPORT BY READING A BOOK ON THE THEORY OF THE GAME SOON BECOMES painfully aware that there is a vast difference between theory and practice. Undoubtedly you will be impressed by this when you attempt to apply the suggestions given in this book to the actual reading of the Bible. As in a game, so in reading: there is no substitute for continuous practice in using the knowledge one has in the situation itself.

If one can add to the reading of a book about his newly embraced sport the experience of watching an expert play it, he will improve his game rapidly. I know a seminary professor who a few years ago followed Byron Nelson, Ben Hogan, and Sammy Snead until his legs would go no farther in the frantic effort to learn how to scale down his extensive damage to the community's well-manicured fairways and greens. His attempt apparently paid off, for he never was ejected from the course!

At the risk of appearing brash in view of the above reference to the performance of an "expert," I am going to attempt to show you how the suggestions made in this book work out when applied to biblical materials. This has been done in part already, for many illustrations have been introduced as we have gone along. But this is not quite like seeing the total effect on a single specimen.

It will be recalled that the books of the Bible were divided into two classes: the unified or substantially unified, and the nonunified. Chapters III and IV dealt with a method of reading the former, and Chapter V with the latter. We shall use as our specimens a book from each group. They are short but fairly representative books: First Thessalonians and Amos.

In applying the reading suggestions to these books I shall attempt to put myself in your place and use the method much as you would use it. There would be little point in digging out of the books results which only a professional biblical scholar could discover. I shall have at my elbow *The Abingdon Bible Commentary*, but the center of attention will be the biblical books themselves.

A. First Thessalonians [1]

1. Reading the letter as a whole is our first step.

We begin with a thoughtful, unhurried reading of the entire letter, with our physical and spiritual eyes wide open. We are to bear in mind the five questions to be answered during the first reading.

The first question (What kind of book is this?) is easy. It is a letter from Paul, Silvanus, and Timothy to the Thessalonians (1:1). As we read, we notice the marks of a genuine letter: a salutation (1:1), friendly remembrances

[1] Parts of this discussion of First Thessalonians appeared in *Interpretation*, April, 1948, pp. 208-17, and are reprinted here by permission.

of past associations (1:1-10), a desire to visit them again (2:17-20), earnest concern for their welfare and relief at hearing good news about them (3:1-10), a desire to help them solve their problems (4:1–5:24), eager solicitation of their interest in the writers' problems (5:25), final instructions and farewell (5:26-28). These things we might put into a letter today. We note that it contains straightforward prose throughout.

The second question (What gives the book its unity?) is more difficult. The center of interest is not a single personality, though there is much in it about Paul. It is not a sermon in the form of a letter, for there is too much personal matter in it. Central are the problems of the Thessalonians. The personal matter is obviously included in the attempt to help them settle certain aspects of their problems. We may say that it is a problem-centered letter.

The third question concerns the logical parts of the letter. In the R.S.V. the revisers have helped us by introducing spaces in several places. We may divide the material as follows:

The salutation (1:1)
Paul's personal relationship with the Thessalonians (1:2–3:13)
A discussion of their problems (4:1–5:24)
The conclusion (5:25-28)

The letter seems to be put together in an orderly manner.

It is hard to answer the fourth question (What reaction does the book stimulate in me?) after one reading. There is much about it that is still unclear. I like the friendly tone. Paul is no plaster saint, but a warm, interested friend. His description of his missionary work at Thessalonica (2:1-12) is most interesting. He is a real pastor—bold enough to tell people what they ought to hear (2:4-6), but gentle and helpful in his manner (2:7-8, 11, 12). His comment about the Jews (2:14-16) seems strange, however, for one so full of love. His practical advice (chapters 4–5) shows that the Christian religion is more than an emotional experience. On the whole I feel that the letter is warm and helpful and will repay careful study, especially since some of the problems of the Thessalonians (discouragement, immortality, laziness) are still with us.

There is plenty to say on the fifth question (What features of the contents are puzzling?). Why doesn't the letter begin "Dear Thessalonians" or "My dear friends at Thessalonica"? Did everybody in Paul's day begin his letters as Paul begins this one? Why does Paul talk so much about himself and seem so worried lest the Thessalonians misunderstand him? Weren't he and they good friends? Why the unkind words about the Jews? How did Satan hinder him from going to see the Thessalonians (2:18)? What exactly did Paul believe about the coming of Christ? What does he mean by such words as "holiness" (3:13) and "sanctification" (4:3; 5:23)?

In the second reading of the whole we are supposed to dig deeper. First of all we are to discover, if possible, the circumstances connected with the writing of the letter. Where were Paul, Silvanus, and Timothy? Was Paul at Athens when he wrote (3:1)? At least he sent Timothy from there. Silvanus must have been somewhere else, because Paul says he was left alone in Athens by Timothy's going. But Timothy has come back to him and brought good news about the Thessalonians (3:6). Was he still in Athens? Clearly this letter is meant to tell the Thessalonians how glad he is to get the good news about them, and to try to help them settle the difficulties they are still facing (3:9-10). There is no clear indication of the date. It was written after he had been in Philippi (2:2), Thessalonica (1:5-10), and Athens (3:1), but nothing more definite is given. Obviously help from A.B.C. will be needed.

The circumstances of the Thessalonians at the time of Paul's writing are reasonably clear. A genuine conversion experience had come to them when Paul was there. It consisted of a deep inner transformation (1:5-6) and a striking change in their outward manner of life (1:7-10). But after he had gone, grievous troubles had set in. Their fellow countrymen had begun to persecute them (2:14; 3:3-4). They were in danger of giving up their Christianity (3:5). The outburst against the Jews (2:14-16) seems to imply that these somehow were instigating the persecution. It appears that someone was spreading lies about Paul—about his motives, his conduct, and the truth of his gospel. He is clearly on the defensive in the letter (2:1-12, 17-19). He wants them to see that he is a true Christian minister and that he really loves them. He seems to be afraid that if they lose faith in him, they will also lose faith in the gospel.

Not only were the Thessalonians emotionally upset by the persecution they were experiencing and by the slander of Paul, but they were intellectually confused. Some Thessalonian church members had died, and their fellow Christians seemed to believe that the deceased would have no part in Christ's kingdom, since they did not live until his return (4:13-18). These immature Christians needed teaching about this and many other things. Furthermore, there were moral problems among them: immorality (4:1-8), laziness (4:10-12), lack of respect for their leaders (5:12), and quarreling (5:13).

The characteristic words, phrases, and ideas appearing in this letter may be briefly noted. A word which helps to give the letter its tender tone is "brethren." The frequency of its occurrence is striking (1:4; 2:1, 9, 14, 17; 3:7; 4:1, 9-10, 13; and 5:1, 4, 12, 14, 25-27). The Thessalonians could scarcely fail to be impressed by this much-repeated indication of Paul's regard for them and the brotherliness of the Christian fellowship. Paul's famous trinity–faith, love, hope–appears twice (1:3; 5:8). Faith and love occur together in 3:6, and faith (1:8; and 3:2, 5, 7, 10), hope (2:19; 4:13), and love (3:12; 4:9, 10; and 5:13) separately. Joy appears in 1:6; 2:19, 20; and 3:9. Other words and expressions are of relatively frequent occurrence: Holy Spirit or Spirit (1:5-6; 4:8; and 5:19); the gospel of God or Christ (1:5; 2:2, 4, 8-9; and 3:2); affliction (1:6; and 3:3-4, 7); wrath (1:10; 2:16; and 5:9. *Cf.* 4:6). Important words are sanctification (4:3; 5:23) and holiness (3:13; 4:4, 7). The coming of Christ is referred to repeatedly (1:10; 2:19; 4:15-17; and 5:2, 4, 23). We shall postpone until later a consideration of the meaning and significance of these words. We are now simply gathering general data.

The emotional quality of the letter has been considered in part, but the extent to which Paul bares his soul is noteworthy. Not only is he intensely concerned about them now (2:17–3:5), but he points out the depth of the love he bore them when he was at Thessalonica (2:7-8, 11). His attitude is well summed up in 2:20 ("For you are our glory and joy") and in 3:8 ("for now we live, if you stand fast in the Lord"). A more solicitous, affectionate letter could hardly have been written.

The obvious divisions of the letter have been given above. But it can be analyzed further. The references to the coming of Christ appear like a refrain, at the end of each chapter, punctuating the book at regular intervals. The chapter divisions have been well made. The structure of the letter is as follows:

- The salutation (1:1)
- Paul's personal relationship with the Thessalonians (1:2–3:13)
  - Thanksgiving for their conversion (1:2-10)
  - Defense of his conduct at Thessalonica and after leaving (2:1-20)
  - The mission of Timothy and its outcome (3:1-13)
- Practical instruction in Christian doctrine and life (4:1–5:24)
- The conclusion (5:25-28)

As a result of these two readings, we now have had sufficient contact with the letter to attempt to formulate its central idea. We might put it thus: "Have confidence in my integrity and in the genuineness of the religious experience you received as a result of my ministry at Thessalonica; press on to a fuller knowledge and experience of the Christian way of life." The adequacy or inadequacy of this summary will become apparent when we have examined the parts and taken the final overview. The central idea appears to be put most sharply in 3:8, 10, 12-13. These verses seem to say, "Stand fast in your newly found faith; and press on to holiness of life!"

We are now in a position to profit from the insights of others who have worked on this letter. We shall know what they are talking about and have pegs on which to hang our information. We can even argue with the "experts," for *we* have *firsthand* knowledge.

From the "Introduction" to First Thessalonians in A.B.C., pages 1263-66, we gain valuable supplementary information. We learn that First Thessalonians is the earliest of Paul's letters in the New Testament, that it was written from Corinth about A.D. 51. We are told a good deal about the city of Thessalonica and are pointed to Acts 17:1–18:17, where another account of Paul's work is to be found. Our conclusions about his reasons for writing are confirmed. Important information about traveling preachers of the period is gained, so that we now understand more clearly why the Thessalonians were suspicious of Paul.

But McCown's analysis of the contents of the letter differs somewhat from ours. Which is better? Why should he divide up 4:1–5:24? Would it not have been better if he had put points two and three together under some such subject as "Personal and Group Problems in the Church at Thessalonica"? Furthermore, his first division contains no mention of Paul's valiant defense of himself in chapter 2. He might well have written "Superscription, Thanksgiving, Defense of his Ministry at Thessalonica, and Prayer."

Our own study of the letter has given us ground to stand on. We are in a position to "test everything" and to "hold fast what is good" (I Thess. 5:21).

2. Next we are to examine the parts.

Our survey of the whole letter through the two readings has led us, as it were, to a peak from which the entire terrain has been surveyed. The next task is to descend and study the lower levels in their relation to the whole. First the telescope and then the microscope.

Our first major division, as I have said, appears to be 1:2–3:13. This part we labeled "Paul's personal relationship with the Thessalonians." We found that it breaks down into several sections, each marked off by the refrainlike reference to the coming of Christ. Our first section is 1:2-10, "Thanksgiving for their conversion." Chapters 2 and 3 each constitute a sectional unit.

We are to ask three questions of 1:2-10 and of each remaining part: Exactly what does it say, and how does it say it? What does it mean? What is its significance for us today? For the purpose of illustration we shall examine here in some detail only 1:2-10.

Under the first question above, we can pass by the inquiry concerning the type of material. We found that the whole book consists of simple, straightforward prose of the kind used in personal letters. The obvious meaning will be the correct one. The writer is not employing poetic metaphor or attempting to conceal his meaning by the use of symbolism.

The next question (Is the section composed of smaller units of material?) calls for a consideration of the structure of the passage. The thought divisions are not immediately obvious, if indeed there are any. Our task is to get beneath the verbiage to the thought skeleton. An examination of the connectives reveals the fact that almost all are subordinating connectives: "for," "so that." Subordinating connectives introduce reasons for previous statements or express results. They tie the material securely together. The thing to do, therefore, is to try to find the central idea (the backbone) of the passage.

The opening statement provides the clue. Everything seems to hang from it in some relationship. "We give thanks to God always for you all." *How* we give thanks is next mentioned: "constantly mentioning you in our prayers." *For what* we give thanks follows and occupies most of the passage: for "your work of faith and labor of love and steadfastness of hope in our Lord Jesus Christ"; and for our assurance that God "has chosen you." The reasons for this assurance are next offered: the peculiar sense of God's presence in power in the life and words of the missionaries when they first preached at Thessalonica (verse 5); and the remarkable conversion experience of the Thessalonians, with its inner and outer fruits (verses 6-10). The passage is thus solidly constructed and is not divisible.

If you are in doubt concerning the structure of a section after you have examined it closely, turn to A.B.C. for help. If your analysis does not agree with the commentator's, argue the point with him. McCown divides 1:2-10 into verses 3-7 and 8-10. When one tests this, he finds that verses 8-10 are quite closely related to verse 7, the latter dealing with the influence of the conversion of the Thessalonians on the areas nearby and the former with its impact on more distant places. Thus there is no large break after verse 7, and the whole may just as well be taken together. Arguing with the commentator will send you more deeply into the heart of the passage than if you meekly accept what you find written in his comments.

The third question involved in observing accurately (What are the important words around which the thought of the unit being studied revolves?) may now be quickly answered. The words needing examination are: "work of faith," "labor of love," "steadfastness of hope," "chosen," "our gospel," "in word, . . . in power . . . in the Holy Spirit . . . with full conviction," "imitators," "the wrath to come," and possibly others.

Puzzling features of the section might include the reason for the defensive attitude in the second half of verse 5, which in a thanksgiving seems out of place; the identification of the territories mentioned in verse 7; the character of the religion of the Thessalonians before their conversion; and the nature of Paul's belief in the coming of Jesus.

From accurate observation, the first major step in the study of a part, we turn next to thoughtful interpretation: What does the passage with its many observed characteristics mean?

Repeated reading will have clarified many obscure points, but some words and phrases will need examination. From A.B.C. we learn that the trinity of expressions in verse 3 may be taken to mean: "Faith produces practical activity, love undertakes toilsome labor, hope supports endurance in view of the imminent return of Christ." No help is given on the meaning of the word "chosen." Obviously the doctrine of divine election is involved here. So important is this doctrine that a more detailed commentary should be consulted, such as *The Epistle of Paul to the Thessalonians*, by William Neil, pages 14-15, or *A Theological Word Book of the Bible*, edited by Alan Richardson, pages 43-44. The extent of your interest will determine the number of resource books you will secure and therefore the number of words you will examine.

The puzzling passages will yield their meaning with a little effort. The larger commentaries will explain that 1:*5b* gives evidence that underlying Paul's thanksgiving there is a veiled argument, which comes clearly to light in chapter 2. The conversion of the Thessalonians proves that Paul is a true minister of God and not a charlatan, as his enemies claim. From the first of the letter he is on the defensive. A.B.C. explains the meaning of "Achaia" and "the wrath to come." On the former religion of the Thessalonians you will have to consult larger commentaries, such as Neil's (pages 27-28).

The central idea of the section (1:2-10) may be stated as follows: Paul gives thanks for conclusive evidence that the Thessalonians have a secure place in God's great redemptive plan. This evidence consists of the striking nature of their conversion experience and the character of its fruits.

Why Paul opens his letter with this kind of thanksgiving can be seen only when one relates the section to the letter as a whole. We found that he was attempting to reassure the persecuted Thessalonians that their faith rested on firm foundations, that the slander circulated by enemies was false. How better could he reassure them than by pointing to the miraculous character of their conversion experience?

The third major question we are to ask of 1:2-10 is, What is its significance for us today? God's word for you in this section will find you where you are. You may be impressed by a number of things in the passage: (1) the deep dedication of consecrated servants of God, who pray unceasingly for the members of their flock and expect much of them; (2) the blessed assurance that Christians have that God loves them and has ordained that they should have a place in his great redemptive plan; (3) the true nature and results of Christian conversion—a receiving of the word of God through the preaching of Spirit-empowered messengers, deep inner joy inspired by the Holy Spirit, the presence in the Christian of the fruits of the

Spirit (faith, love, and hope) and the practical results in daily life to which they lead, the radical change in one's outward manner of life, and the influence of converts on others; (4) the strange occurrence of joy in the midst of affliction; and (5) the glorious hope for the future cherished by Christians.

You may want to study the question of the relationship between a person's background and the nature of his conversion experience, so that you may know to what extent the Thessalonians' experience may be duplicated in your life and in the churches of modern America. You may wish to discuss this with your minister and with other members of your church. You will certainly be led to deep searching of heart. Out of it may come incalculable blessing to you, your family, your church, and your world.

3. Our final step is to re-view the whole letter.

It is to be regretted that we cannot proceed here section by section through First Thessalonians, so that the rich content of the letter might be before us as we attempt the final synthesis. It must suffice to make a few summarizing remarks about the remaining sections. In chapter 2 the center of interest shifts from "you" to "we," as Paul reminds the readers of the character of his ministry among them. He points out that it was a courageous (2:2), sound (2:3-4), uncompromising (2:4-5), selfless and self-giving (2:6-8), self-supporting (2:9), blameless (2:10), and patient (2:11) ministry. The slander of his enemies was belied by the facts. It is small wonder that the results at Thessalonica were so remarkable. With more ministers of this sort in America the impact of the church on the nation and the world might rival or surpass that made by the Thessalonian Christians.

Chapter 3 continues Paul's defense of his conduct down

to the moment of writing. It is now perfectly clear that the whole of chapters 1–3 (except for the salutation) is an extended defense of the validity of his gospel and his personal integrity. He says in effect, "Do not be alienated from God's redemptive plan, in which you now have a part, by the malicious attacks of our common enemies. You are on the right track. Keep on! There is much spiritual territory yet to be possessed."

The "practical" section of the letter (4:1–5:24) presents fewer difficulties of interpretation than the apologetic. The clue to the contents of this section is given in 3:10*b* and 3:13. Paul wishes to "supply what is lacking in your faith," and to "establish your hearts unblamable in holiness." A study of each problem discussed here from the standpoint of the Christian standard laid down by Paul, the appeals used by him in the attempt to motivate his readers to seek to attain those standards, and the practical measures by which progress can be made will be well worth the effort.

With this brief summary of the remaining "parts" we shall attempt a final synthesis.

The central idea: Your religion is sound; go on to a full realization of its potentialities.

I. Your conversion experience demonstrates its validity (chapter 1).

II. The character and conduct of your spiritual leaders proves its validity (chapters 2–3).

III. Therefore, press on toward the full realization of the Christian quality of life (holiness, entire sanctification) (chapters 4–5).

Several special themes of the letter should be investigated: the teaching concerning the coming of Christ, the qualities of spirit that should characterize the Christian, the pattern of conduct for personal and church life, and the methods by which the goals may be attained. In connection with the first theme mentioned, Second Thessalonians should be considered.

We may bypass here the final relating of the message of the letter to the historical situation and the study of remaining obscurities in the light of the whole, as sufficiently covered for our present purposes, and conclude with the contribution of the letter as a whole to our individual and corporate lives. We ought not to leave First Thessalonians until we have brought our lives, our church, and our society under its judgment. The letter offers some teachings of great significance:

1. True Christian conversion consists of an inner transformation and an outer manifestation—a faith, love, and hope that lead to practical Christian activity. It is not simply intellectual persuasion.

2. Such conversion results from faithful preaching and righteous living of selfless servants of God.

3. Conversion is but the beginning. Establishment in holiness of life is the goal toward which every Christian must press on. Since it is God's will, the faithful pursuit of this quality of life is not optional but mandatory.

4. Holiness of life, as set forth here, consists of sexual purity, brotherly love (mutual helpfulness, appreciation, forgiveness), industriousness, spiritual alertness, thankfulness and prayerfulness, the ability to discriminate between right and wrong, and power to do the right. It is not a vague inner feeling but a quality of living.

5. God and men must work together to bring about the

desired result. Not only are the latter to be diligent personally, but they are to help one another, knowing that what God demands, he is able and willing to supply.

B. The Book of Amos

Our rather full application to First Thessalonians of the method of reading unified books will make necessary a briefer treatment of Amos. We shall attempt to see only in broad outlines how the suggestions for reading non-unified books work out.

1. A perusal of the book of Amos discloses considerable evidence concerning the prophet's times. In 1:1 and 7:9-10 we learn that his prophecies were uttered during the reigns of Uzziah, king of Judah, and Jeroboam, king of Israel. More specifically, the coming of the word of the Lord to him is put "two years before the earthquake" (1:1).[2]

We learn that there was a royal sanctuary at Bethel, presided over by a priest by the name of Amaziah, who considered it his duty to protect Jeroboam's interests (7:12-13). Evidently the priests and the kings worked closely together. There were also sanctuaries at Gilgal (4:4; 5:5) and Dan (8:14).

Religion at the sanctuaries consisted of daily ceremonies in which various types of sacrifices and offerings were presented (4:4-5), and of occasional great festal gatherings at which "fatted beasts" were offered (5:22) and singing, eating, drinking, and even sexual intercourse indulged in (5:23; 2:7-8). Idolatry apparently was not unknown (5:26).

[2] The date of the earthquake is not known, but A.B.C. points out that it must have been a very severe one, for it was remembered long afterward (see Zech. 14:5).

Economically Israel was relatively prosperous. The upper class "built houses of hewn stone" (5:11), planted "pleasant vineyards" (5:11), lolled on "beds of ivory" (6:4), and feasted, drank, and anointed themselves with costly oils (6:4-6). The base women of Samaria debauched themselves and their husbands (4:1). Merchants could scarcely await the expiration of the Sabbath and the day of the new moon, so eager were they to be on with their money-making (8:4-5). But in the midst of prosperity there was poverty. The wealthy grew richer by exploiting the poor through sharp lending practices (2:8*a*), fines (2:8*b*), forced taxes (5:11), dishonest sales practices (8:5-6), and bribery of judges in court (2:6-7*a*; 5:7, 12; 6:12).

Around opulent, decadent Israel were corrupt neighbors who had little regard for basic human rights: Damascus, Gaza, Tyre, Edom, Ammon, Moab (1:3–2:3). And farther away were predatory Assyria and Egypt, waiting to plunder the palaces of Israel (3:9-11).

Supplementary material from A.B.C., pages 775-76, offers valuable insights into the economic, social, and religious aspects of village and country life in the time of Amos, a clear summary of the sins of his age (with special attention to Canaanite influence on Israel's religion), and details of the political situation. The discussion is particularly illuminating because our curiosity has been aroused by references discovered in the book of Amos itself. And we are now able to check on our own powers of observation.

2. A survey of the book discloses the following sequence of materials:

a) Title and theme (1:1-2).

b) The coming doom of surrounding nations and of Israel (1:3–2:16). That this passage is a unit is clearly evident from the stereotyped form throughout. Note 1:3, 6, 9, 11, 13; 2:1, 4, 6; and the contents of each oracle.

c) The sins of Israel and the coming destruction (3:1–6:14). These oracles are introduced by "Hear this word" (3:1; 4:1; 5:1) and "Woe" (5:18; 6:1). The subject matter throughout alternates between a recital of Israel's sins and description of the coming devastation.

d) The prophet's visions and the messages derived from them (7:1–9:15). Prominent is the phrase "Thus the Lord God showed me" (7:1, 4, 7; 8:1). In the midst of this portion a piece concerning Amos' encounter with Amaziah has been inserted (7:10-17), apparently because of the mention of Jeroboam in 7:9.

At the beginning of your study of biblical books the contents may seem like a jumble of words without any organization. But keep looking for the patterns that hold them together. When you turn to A.B.C. for help, test out the analysis there given to see why it was made thus. You will grow rapidly in ability to see for yourself.

3. Relate the various portions of the book to their proper historical background. This point is the hardest of all. Here scholars differ widely, but for full understanding—and often for any kind of understanding—an attempt must be made.

It would be nice if the person who put the book together had arranged the oracles and the autobiographical and biographical materials in chronological sequence. We could then fit the prophet's life and words together. But, lacking this, we must do the best we can.

a) Messages from the Lord prior to Amos' call (7:1-6). Since Amos through his intercession changed the mind of the Lord from punishment to mercy, it is evident that these two experiences preceded his prophetic ministry. This was marked throughout with the certainty of coming destruction.

b) The call to prophesy (3:3-8; 7:14-15). These passages emphasize the divine origin of his call. The point of 3:3-8 is that every effect must have a corresponding cause. So Amos' prophesying has its cause—the command of the Lord. He points out that because of his birth and background such activity was foreign to him.

c) Proclamation at Samaria, Gilgal, and Bethel. Most of the oracles contained in the book apparently were uttered at these places. Since they are not presented in the book in a chronological or logical order, it is impossible to assign them with any certainty to exact places and times. It is commonly believed that Amos' ministry lasted two or three months.

d) The encounter with Amaziah at Bethel (7:10-17). In view of Amos' unyielding attitude when he was forbidden by Amaziah to prophesy in Israel (7:14-17), it is possible that he was jailed or even martyred. The ominous reference to the notification of Jeroboam concerning Amos' treasonous words might point to official condemnation. We simply do not know how Amos met his end.

e) Later additions to the book of Amos. The book has experienced additions here and there to bring it up to date for later times. Scholars are largely agreed that 9:9-15 is such an addition. It accords poorly, as far as content is concerned, with the fiery proclamations of Amos, and it lacks the literary qualities that mark his oracles.[3] One scholar thinks that nearly half of the text of Amos is from later hands,[4] but this is surely extreme.

The kind of historical reconstruction here undertaken cannot be done by a beginner. Use your commentaries and larger introductions to the Old Testament for help. Maximum illumination on a prophet's life and work comes by such chronological rearrangement.

4. Amos' words are so graphic that it is not difficult to

[3] See A.B.C., p. 783.

[4] Rolland Emerson Wolfe, *Meet Amos and Hosea* (New York: Harper & Bros., 1945), p. *xvii*.

imagine the circumstances under which they were spoken. We can see the shepherd and dresser of sycamore trees, crude in dress, unpolished in manner, appearing suddenly at a gathering of fashionable ladies of Samaria and, with a storm on his face and thunder in his voice, denouncing the fat "cows of Bashan" who use the poor and their wealthy husbands to gratify their insatiable desires (4:1). Again, we see him mixing with a throng of merrymakers at Gilgal and, in the midst of the ceremonies and singing and feasting, rising and silencing the crowd with fiery denunciations (4:4-5; 5:21-24). And who could not write a dramatic skit on his tilt with Amaziah? Imagination is used to a marked degree in R. E. Wolfe's reconstruction of the career of Amos.[5] If imaginative reconstructions are kept within the bounds of historical probability, the result is all to the good.

5. The central notes in Amos' preaching are easy to find. Few portions of the Old Testament are so lucid and pungent. He was a master in the use of language. It is inconceivable that his hearers went away wondering what he had said, so apt are his figures of speech, so simple his style, and so arresting his ideas. We cannot include here everything of importance that he said, but we may list his greatest conceptions.

a) The God of Israel is the Lord of the whole earth. Though he stands in a special relationship to Israel (3:2), his interest and activity are directed also toward the Ethiopians, Philistines, and Syrians. He gave homelands to them as well as to Israel (9:7). He not only holds the people of Israel accountable for their actions but also their enemies, for his jurisdiction extends over all nations (1:3–2:3).

[5] *Ibid., passim.*

b) He is a God of righteousness. Though Amos sees him as a God of might who can handle the nations as he will, Amos is chiefly impressed by the fact of his righteousness (rightness). There is nothing capricious, cruel, or unethical about him. God and the good are closely identified (5:4, 14). He is forever against nations and individuals who do wrong. His chief complaint against the people of Israel is that "they do not know how to do right" (3:10).

c) God's requirements are moral, not ceremonial. Elaborate sacrificial rites at the sanctuaries are obnoxious to him (5:21-24), even though they are delighted in by the people (4:5). What he wants of men is unfailing justice in their relationships with each other (5:24; 2:6-7; 4:1; and 8:4-6). Sin, for Amos, is not a failure to worship in the right way; it is a repudiation of fundamental principles of right in daily living.

d) God supports those who do right and punishes those who do evil. Those who seek the good (God) will live (5:4, 6, 14). Those who practice unrighteousness will be destroyed (1:3–2:16; 5:16; 6:4-14; etc.). God has no favorites, and he makes no exceptions. Israel has no special claim on him and will get off no more easily than other nations that have violated fundamental principles of morality. The "day of the Lord" (the day when God judges), instead of bringing victory and vindication to Israel, will result in destruction and humiliation (5:18-20).

After you have drawn up your conclusions concerning the central emphases in the preaching of Amos from an examination of the book itself, you should compare your results with those of H. Wheeler Robinson in A.B.C. (page 776). If you will take my summary above and make this comparison, you will note that Robinson stresses several points not covered in my discussion. And the contrary is also true. Furthermore, you will see that he has related the teaching as a whole to the historical situation in which it was set forth. His discussion thus supplies valuable supplementary material.

6. An estimate of the contribution of Amos to the life and destiny of his nation cannot be arrived at from a knowledge of his book alone. The cross references at the bottom of each page will help you see what passages are quoted in the New Testament and to what extent Amos and other prophets discussed the same or similar subjects. By themselves, however, these references will not tell you much concerning his influence on his prophetic successors. Influence is very difficult to measure.

Here you will have to draw from the best secondary sources. H. Wheeler Robinson says little in his "Introduction" about Amos' contribution. However, in his article on "The Religion of Israel" (A.B.C. pages 165-76) help is to be found, and especially in the article by A. C. Knudson on "The Old Testament Conception of God" (A.B.C. pages 158-64). From these discussions, and from others you may read, you will come to see that "Amos marks the beginning of a new era in the history of religion,"[6] and that Jesus could not have done his work without the foundation of ethical monotheism (the belief in one God, who is good and demands right conduct of all men) laid by Amos and other prophets after him.

7. There is so much in Amos that is of great importance for our times that one hardly knows where to begin and certainly not where to stop. A recent writer has said,

> No one can ponder the prophecies of Amos without discovering how directly they bear upon the problems of our modern world. Amos preaches today as truly as when he lived. The writings of all these prophets exhibit a unique timelessness. For they deal not only with the issues of their day but with the

[6] R. H. Pfeiffer, *Introduction to the Old Testament* (New York: Harper & Bros., 1941), p. 580.

fundamental problems of life. The message of Amos, if heeded and obeyed, would solve for us of today problems that vex and disturb us.[7]

Instead of attempting a statement, let me throw out a few questions for thought, the kind of questions you should pose to yourself in reading the Prophets. To what extent would Amos' condemnation of Israel be applicable to present-day America? What about the conception held widely today that God bears a special relationship to particular peoples and is therefore bound to support them against their enemies? In the light of the teaching of Amos, how would God's purpose for the world be affected by the destruction of the democratic Western powers by their Eastern opponents? Does God actually punish individuals and nations for their sins? If so, how? Is it correct to think that God wants only personal and national morality and is wholly indifferent to forms of corporate worship? What about the strong trend toward ritualistic worship in certain denominations of our time?

If you will plunge deeply into these and other questions that will occur to you as you work through Amos, you will find this ancient prophet speaking mightily to you and your contemporaries.

[7] Raymond Calkins, *The Modern Message of the Minor Prophets* (New York: Harper & Bros., 1947), p. 24.

CHAPTER SEVEN

Programs of Reading

THE BIBLE HAS BEEN READ FROM EVERY CONCEIVABLE POINT OF VIEW. THE CHURCH HAS SEARCHED THROUGH ITS pages for arguments to support dogmas, and many sectarians of today have gathered out proof-texts for use in the hour of verbal battle. Since the Renaissance, and especially in the first third of the twentieth century, literary men have praised its qualities and sought to excite students about its superb examples of literary art. Historians have pored over its contents. By breaking the books down into their sources and arranging them chronologically, they have found exciting data for writing the history of the Near East, and especially the history of Israel. Scientists have peered into it for light on the development of mankind in the areas of their respective interests. Philosophers and religious educators have traced the growth of the moral concepts of the Hebrews from their roots in primitive nomadic life to their flowering in the New Testament and the Christian church.

Our purpose in approaching the Bible will largely determine how we will read it: where we will begin, in what sequence we will read, and what we will look for and discover. Every thoughtful approach will result in some solid values. It should be stated frankly and flatly, however, that those who view the Bible as of significance chiefly for the historical information and reading pleasure it offers do it little honor. In fact, they really cannot understand it, for they err concerning its fundamental nature.

If what was said in Axiom VI [1] is true, the purpose of the Bible is to "bring men *to* Christ, to build them up *in* Christ, and to send them out *for* Christ." This conception of its purpose is deeply rooted in the Bible itself. In John 5:39-40 Jesus is represented as saying to the Jews, "You search the scriptures, because you think that in them you have eternal life; and it is they that bear witness to me; yet you refuse to come to me that you may have life." The classical statement of the Bible's purpose (though the writer of course had in mind only the Old Testament) is II Tim. 3:14-17. It is said here that the Scriptures (1) lead to salvation through faith in Christ, (2) are useful in teaching, in reproof, in correcting faults, and in training in uprightness, and (3) equip a person for every good work. The writers of the Bible viewed themselves not as historians, scientists, or literary specialists, but as bearers of a divine message—that God was active in the experiences of the people of Israel to bring about the redemption of mankind. It was their desire to witness to the wonderful acts of God.

We read the Bible best, then, when we read it in a way that will allow it to tell us most clearly its story of redemption. Jesus and the early church saw this story spelled out

[1] Pp. 27-30.

before them in the Old Testament, and they brought their lives into line with God's gracious purposes there revealed. Thus they became a part of the story, indeed the climax of it. We can do no better than to read the Scriptures from the standpoint taken by them.

The first disciples began, as we must begin, with the fact of Jesus. Peter's sermon in the house of Cornelius (Acts 10:34-43) began there—with Jesus of Nazareth as God's word to men, a word spoken in his Spirit-empowered deeds, in his death, and in his resurrection. He affirmed that Jesus has been ordained by God as the Judge and Saviour of all men. "To him all the prophets bear witness" (10:43). It is noteworthy that Peter did not begin with the prophets, but ended with them. The early Christians believed in Jesus as Saviour not so much because he fulfilled the prophecies of the Old Testament as because the prophecies of the Old Testament gained meaning after they had looked long and intimately at him. To put it in another way, they did not so much interpret Jesus by the Old Testament as the Old Testament by Jesus.

Two programs of reading are set forth below, a longer and a shorter. You will note that both proceed in line with the position taken above about the Bible's purpose. They begin with Jesus as he is revealed in the Gospels. Next his impact on and through the primitive Christian communities (as seen in the Acts of the Apostles) is considered. This lays the ground for the interpretation of Jesus made by Paul in behalf of the churches of the Greco-Roman world (in the letters of Paul). The testimony of other interpreters of Jesus and Christianity (Hebrews, the Pastoral and the General Epistles) follows. Revelation is reserved for treatment with Daniel at the end of the programs of reading.

It is believed that these books can be understood best in the light of a knowledge of the whole Bible.

Moving into the Old Testament from the vantage point gained by reading the New, you will be in a position to see how God worked in the persons and events of Hebrew history to bring Jesus and the Christian church into being. Standing closest to Jesus among the figures of the Old Testament are the prophets. Jesus was conscious that in a very real sense he was treading in their footsteps. We shall want to know how he compares with and how he differs from them, and what their contribution to him was. Next we shall consider the Psalms. The early church felt that God's saving purpose and activity were plainly declared in many of them (Luke 24:44), and we know how intimately Jesus knew them. The wisdom books, Proverbs and Job, may be introduced here, since in some respects they are akin to the Psalms. Their treatment of the doctrine of retribution is necessary background for understanding the suffering of Jesus. Next we shall consider the historical narratives, Genesis through Nehemiah. The early church believed that even in these books the divine footprints leading to the cross could be traced (Luke 24:27, 44; John 5:46). And finally we shall look forward with the writers of Daniel and Revelation to the triumph of the saints of the Most High, who will receive the kingdom and reign in blessed fellowship with their victorious Lord forevermore.

Though the approach here outlined is Christ-centered, you will not allegorize the Old Testament if you will bear in mind the rules of interpretation set forth in Chapter II. We are to look for evidences of the divine activity culminating in Christ Jesus. We are not to import the historical Jesus into passages of the Old Testament. Beginning with the flower of wondrous beauty, we pass to its effects on its beholders, and then to an inquiry into the way in which this blessed "miracle" came to be. From what roots and stock did it grow?

A. The Longer Program of Reading

Mark
Matthew
John
Luke-Acts
First Thessalonians
Second Thessalonians
Galatians
First Corinthians
Second Corinthians
  Chaps. 10–13
  Chaps. 1–9
Romans
Philemon
Philippians
Colossians
Ephesians
Hebrews
First Peter
First John
James
Titus
First Timothy
Second Timothy
Jude
Second Peter

Amos
Hosea
Isaiah (1–39, especially 1–12)
Micah
Jeremiah (1–45)
Habakkuk
Isaiah (40-66, especially 40-55)
Haggai
Zechariah (1–8)
Malachi
Ruth
Jonah
Psalms[2]
Proverbs (1–9)
Job
Genesis
Exodus
Leviticus (Scan only)
Numbers
Deuteronomy
Joshua
Judges
First Samuel
Second Samuel
First Kings
Second Kings
Ezra
Nehemiah
Daniel
Revelation

[2] The following psalms in the various types are suggested for reading:
Hymns: 150, 46, 84, 122, 103, 93, 96, 97, 2, 72, 110, 65, 8, 19, 104

B. The Shorter Program

Mark
Luke-Acts
First Thessalonians
Galatians
First Corinthians
Romans
Philippians
Ephesians
First Peter
First John
Titus
Second Timothy

Amos
Hosea
Isaiah (1–12)
Jeremiah (1–25)
Isaiah (40–55)
Ruth
Jonah
Psalms[3]
Job
Genesis
Exodus (1–24. Scan 25–40.)
Numbers (10:11–14:45; 20:1–25:18)
Deuteronomy (1–11)
Joshua (1–12)
Samuel-Kings (Dip in here and there to sample the stories.)
Nehemiah
Daniel or Revelation

Liturgies: 15, 24, 100, 136, 95, 121
Laments of the People of Israel: 44, 90, 137
Psalms About the King: 20, 61
Songs of Individual Thanksgiving: 23, 32, 34, 139, 146
Prayers of the Falsely Accused, Sick, and Penitent: 42, 43, 27, 57, 22, 71, 51, 130
Songs of Trust and of Wisdom: 91, 37, 73

[3] The following psalms in the various types are suggested for reading:
Hymns: 46, 84, 103, 65, 8, 19
Liturgies: 15, 24, 95, 121
Laments of the People of Israel: 90, 137
Songs of Individual Thanksgiving: 23, 32, 139
Prayers of the Falsely Accused, Sick, and Penitent: 42, 43, 27, 51, 130
Songs of Trust and of Wisdom: 91, 37, 73

CHAPTER EIGHT

Resources for Reading

BOOKS ABOUT THE BIBLE ARE LEGION. THIS MAY BE EITHER GOOD OR BAD, DEPENDING ON YOUR POINT OF VIEW. It is good that the Bible is thought so important that people cannot help writing about it. It is bad if the great number of such books is symptomatic of a deep-seated feeling that the average man cannot read and understand the Bible but must be told what is there by an "expert." Before his death Martin Luther, who himself wrote many books about the Bible, became apprehensive concerning the growing number of such books. He said:

> The Bible is now buried under so many commentaries, that the text is nothing regarded. . . . Never will the writings of mortal man in any respect equal the sentences inspired by God. We must yield the place of honour to the prophets and the apostles, keeping ourselves prostrate at their feet as we listen to their teachings. I would not have those who read my books, in these stormy times, devote one moment to them which they would otherwise have consecrated to the Bible.[1]

[1] *The Table Talk or Familiar Discourse of Martin Luther*, trans. by William Hazlitt (London: David Bogue, 1848), p. 369.

It can hardly be doubted that Luther sensed a real danger. Many modern books about the Bible were written for lazy minds, for people who are used to "digests" of one sort or another and whose minds have become stunted by their aversion to firsthand study. Our fathers grew mentally hardy on the Bible. They came to a certain maturity of judgment and independence of spirit by probing deeply into it. It was not beyond them, and it is not beyond us, if we are willing to pay the price they paid.

The best books about the Bible, then, are those that help us most in reading and interpreting it for ourselves. This point of view has been before us throughout the present volume. It explains the constant insistence on using A.B.C. and other secondary sources for background, clarification of the text, supplementation, and correction, but not as a substitute for personal digging in the primary source.

An attempt has been made in the following bibliography to list only books that may be used understandingly by a layman and which will help him in *direct* Bible study. They are listed under each caption in the order of usefulness in connection with the reading procedures set forth in this book.

The Text of the Bible

The Holy Bible: Revised Standard Version. New York: Thomas Nelson & Sons, 1952. See also *Nelson's Complete Concordance of the Revised Standard Version Bible.*

Commentaries on the Bible

Eiselen, Lewis, Downey (eds.). *The Abingdon Bible Commentary*. New York and Nashville: Abingdon-Cokesbury Press, 1929. The best one-volume commentary on the entire Bible. Numerous articles.

Davies, Richardson, Wallis (ed.). *The Twentieth Century Bible Commentary*. New York: Harper and Bros., rev. ed., 1955.

A reliable, brief commentary on the entire Bible, with general articles, a chronological table, maps, bibliographies.

W. K. Lowther Clarke. *Concise Bible Commentary*. New York: The Macmillan Co., 1953. Embodies the results of forty years of work. Background articles especially helpful. Apocryphal books included.

Marsh, Richardson, Smith (eds.). *Torch Bible Commentaries.* London: Student Christian Movement Press, 1948 ——. A simply written series, stressing religious and theological values. Brief.

James Moffatt (ed.). *The Moffatt New Testament Commentaries.* New York: Harper & Bros., 1928-1950. A series of commentaries of high quality on Moffatt's translation of the New Testament.

George A. Buttrick (ed.). *The Interpreter's Bible.* New York and Nashville: Abingdon-Cokesbury Press, 1951——. A monumental work of scholarship. Currently appearing volume by volume. Brilliant exposition in simple language.

Bible Dictionaries

Madeleine S. Miller and J. Lane Miller. *Harper's Bible Dictionary*. New York: Harper and Bros., 1952. Hundreds of biblical subjects arranged alphabetically and discussed in brief articles. Easily read, up-to-date, profusely illustrated.

J. D. Davis and H. S. Gehman. *The Westminster Dictionary of the Bible*. Philadelphia: Westminster Press, 1944. Same general content as preceding book but written from a more conservative point of view.

Atlases of Bible Lands

H. G. May and C. C. McCown. *A Remapping of the Bible World*. New York: Thomas Nelson and Sons, 1949. An inexpensive booklet of biblical maps by first-rate scholars. No explanatory text.

G. E. Wright and F. V. Filson. *The Westminster Historical Atlas to the Bible*. Philadelphia: Westminster Press, rev. ed., 1956.

Excellent, up-to-date maps of the various periods of biblical history, with highly informative explanatory text.

Lexicon

Alan Richardson (ed.). *A Theological Word Book of the Bible.* New York: The Macmillan Co., 1951. An indispensable tool for arriving at the meaning of biblical words.

Introductions to the Old Testament

W. O. E. Oesterley and T. H. Robinson. *An Introduction to the Books of the Old Testament.* New York: The Macmillan Co., 1934. A discussion by widely recognized British authorities of the authorship, date, contents, meaning, etc., of each book of the Old Testament.

J. E. McFadyen. *Introduction to the Old Testament.* New York: The Macmillan Co., 1933. Same content in general as the above book but somewhat less detailed. Reliable, readable.

H. Wheeler Robinson. *The Old Testament: Its Making and Meaning.* New York and Nashville: Abingdon-Cokesbury Press, 1937. A simply written discussion of the way in which the books of the Old Testament came to be. Highly enlightening.

Introductions to the New Testament

F. V. Filson. *Opening the New Testament.* Philadelphia: Westminster Press, 1952. A sound, popular account of the writing and value of each New Testament book.

E. J. Goodspeed. *An Introduction to the New Testament.* Chicago: University of Chicago Press, 1937. The well-known former University of Chicago professor conducts the reader through each New Testament book to explain its origin and meaning. Easy to read.

E. F. Scott. *The Literature of the New Testament.* New York: Columbia University Press, 1932. A book-by-book discussion of the New Testament by a widely known authority. Long a standard work in the field.

Richard G. Heard. *An Introduction to the New Testament.* New York: Harper and Bros., 1950. Emphasizes religious and theological values of the New Testament. Especially valuable material on the Gospels and the life of Jesus.

The Nature and Meaning of the Bible

H. H. Rowley. *The Relevance of the Bible.* New York: The Macmillan Co., 1944. A splendid discussion of the problems of the inspiration, authority, and significance of the Bible. Some attention to major biblical themes. Highly recommended.

Alan Richardson. *A Preface to Bible Study.* Philadelphia: The Westminster Press, 1944. A highly rewarding book on attitudes and objectives in studying the Bible. Not primarily a book on method of study.

B. W. Anderson. *Rediscovering the Bible.* New York: Association Press, 1951. An ideal book for people who are bothered by many of the problems in the Bible. Biblical religion comes alive in this book.

———. *Understanding the Old Testament.* Englewood Cliffs, New Jersey: Prentice-Hall, Inc., 1957. A view of the Old Testament against its historical background. Superbly done.

H. C. Kee and F. W. Young. *Understanding the New Testament.* Englewood Cliffs, New Jersey: Prentice-Hall, Inc., 1957. A companion volume to the one above.

The History of the English Bible

Herbert Gordon May. *Our English Bible in the Making.* Philadelphia: Westminster Press, 1952. A reliable, nontechnical account of the making of the many English versions of the Bible (including the R.S.V.).

Reading Suggestions and Questions for Discussion

The Preface

1. Read the Preface to the R.S.V. and answer the following questions:

How is the R.S.V. related to the King James Version?

What are the chief defects in the King James Version?

In what ways are present-day scholars in a better position to produce a more accurate version of the Bible than were the scholars of the time of King James?

2. If you would like more information about the R.S.V., secure the pamphlets mentioned on p. 9, note 3.

3. For an interesting, brief description of the history of the English Bible and the many versions now current (except for the R.S.V.) see A.B.C., pp. 80-87.

Chapter I. The Basic Nature of the Bible

1. See A.B.C., pp. 15-18, for information on the following:

The meaning of the word "Bible."

The meaning of "Old Testament" and "New Testament."

The arrangement of the books of the Old and New Testaments.

The types of literature in the Bible and their major characteristics.

2. What do the sixty-six books of the Bible have in common? In what sense do they form *one* book?

3. On the subject of the inspiration of the Bible read A.B.C., pp. 26-31.

What characteristics of the Bible indicate that in some sense it is a human book?

What characteristics indicate that it is also a divine book?

4. Which of the Axioms listed in Chapter I relate to its divine and which to its human aspects?

Chapter II. How to Understand the Bible

1. What types of mistakes in interpreting the Bible is the average reader apt to make?

2. What do you think of the Roman Catholic position that the church alone can give a final, authoritative explanation of the Bible's meaning?

3. It is sometimes said that "higher critics" are trying to destroy faith in the Bible as the Word of God. Is biblical criticism necessarily destructive? See A.B.C., pp. 129-33 and pp. 885-90.

4. Explain what is meant by the historical context, the immediate context, and the remote context; and show why attention to the context is important in interpretation.

5. Why is it important to know that much of the Old Testament is poetry, and that it be printed as such in our English Bibles?

6. To what extent are personal commitment and mature Christian experience of significance in correctly interpreting the Bible? What part does the Holy Spirit play in the work of interpretation?

Chapter III. Reading a Book as a Whole

1. What is wrong and what is right in the way the average Christian reads the Bible?

2. What is meant by "unified and substantially unified" books and "nonunified" books? Why is it not possible to use exactly the same procedure in reading both kinds?

3. Why is reading books as wholes important? See the remarks on this in A.B.C., p. 4.

4. Test out your understanding of the directions for reading a whole book by applying them to the book of Ruth, Jonah, or Nehemiah. For checking on your results use A.B.C. or one of the introductions to the Old Testament listed on p. 149. Remember that not every direction will apply equally well to each book of the Bible.

Chapter IV. Examining the Parts and Re-Viewing the Whole

1. Examine the following passages and explain why the paragraph

divisions and the chapter divisions do not coincide: Exod. 6:28–7:7; I Sam. 6:19–7:2; Mark 8:34–9:1; II Cor. 1:23–2:4.

2. Check the spacing in the text of the following books to see how the revisers have helped you in dividing them into parts: John, Romans, Ephesians, Colossians, First Thessalonians.

3. Luke 1:5–2:52 will offer you a good specimen on which to try out the suggestions for reading a "part." The type of material there is significant, it divides easily into smaller units (episodes), it presents features that require one to search out meanings and evaluate carefully, and it is full of rewarding material. You will not be able to use all the steps in the reading procedure, because you will not have "surveyed the whole." Your purpose should be to understand the steps in the procedure, not to study the passage exhaustively. Use A.B.C. as needed. You may want to read parts of the article "The Miracles of the New Testament" (pp. 921-30).

Chapter V. Reading the Nonunified Books

1. For further information about Israel's early folk literature see A.B.C., p. 21 ("Pre-Biblical Fragments and Quotations") and p. 155 ("Folk-Poetry").

2. Few subjects in biblical study are more fascinating than the experiences and teachings of Israel's great prophets. In order to broaden your knowledge of the prophetic movement, read the brief treatment of the prophetic literature in A.B.C., pp. 150-53. What suggestions do you find for helping *us* distinguish between the true and false prophets of *our* day?

3. In Jer. 36 the writing of a prophetic book is described. Read this dramatic chapter. Why was the scroll written, what apparently did it contain, and what became of it? For information about writing and writing materials see A.B.C., pp. 99-101. Some scholars think the second scroll (verse 32) forms the basis of chapters 1–25 of our present book of Jeremiah. You may wish to scan these chapters for a general idea of their contents.

4. Select one psalm (preferably a short one) from each of the major types for reading. See if you can find in each some of the marks of its type. Which type do you like best? Why?

Chapter VI. Applying the Methods of Reading

You will not gain from this chapter what you ought to gain if you simply *read* it. It is intended that you should work through it step by step with your Bible before you, checking every reference in First Thessalonians and Amos, weighing every conclusion, and even arguing with me over my results. You also should consult A.B.C. where needed.

Ideally you should first use entirely by yourself the reading procedures appropriate to each book, so that you might compare your results with mine. This, however, would require considerable time. But by all means check closely every process and conclusion to make sure you understand what is being done.

Chapters VII and VIII. Programs of Reading and Resources for Reading

1. Why should the Bible be read as a book of religion rather than of history or science?
2. Why should we begin with the Gospels and not with Genesis?
3. In what way may books about the Bible, if improperly used, undermine the fundamental purpose of the Bible?
4. Good books about the Bible (such as those by Anderson, Richardson, and Rowley) will broaden your horizons and deepen your insights in your direct reading of the Bible. Dip into them now and then and return to them as you encounter in the Bible problems with which they deal.